# MARTIAL'S EPIGRAMS

# MARTIAL'S EPIGRAMS

A SELECTION

Translated and with an Introduction by

# Garry Wills

VIKING

VIKING
Published by the Penguin Group
Penguin Group (USA) Inc., 375 Hudson Street, New York, New York 10014,
U.S.A. • Penguin Group (Canada), 90 Eglinton Avenue East, Suite 700, Toronto,
Ontario, Canada M4P 2Y3 (a division of Pearson Penguin Canada Inc.) •
Penguin Books Ltd, 80 Strand, London WC2R 0RL, England • Penguin Ire-
land, 25 St. Stephen's Green, Dublin 2, Ireland (a division of Penguin Books
Ltd) • Penguin Books Australia Ltd, 250 Camberwell Road, Camberwell,
Victoria 3124, Australia (a division of Pearson Australia Group Pty Ltd) • Pen-
guin Books India Pvt Ltd, 11 Community Centre, Panchsheel Park, New
Delhi–110 017, India • Penguin Group (NZ), 67 Apollo Drive, Rosedale,
North Shore 0632, New Zealand (a division of Pearson New Zealand
Ltd) • Penguin Books (South Africa) (Pty) Ltd, 24 Sturdee Avenue, Rose-
bank, Johannesburg 2196, South Africa

Penguin Books Ltd, Registered Offices:
80 Strand, London WC2R 0RL, England

First published in 2007 by Viking Penguin,
a member of Penguin Group (USA) Inc.

10   3   5   7   9   10   8   6   4   2

ISBN 978-0-670-02039-3

Printed in the United States of America
Set in Caslon Book BE with ITC Founders Caslon 12
Designed by Daniel Lagin

To D. B. Shackleton Bailey
*Martialissimo*

# CONTENTS

# MARTIAL'S EPIGRAMS

# INTRODUCTION

## Rome's Gossip Columnist

Martial–Marcus Valerius Martialis, c. 40–c. 102 CE–was a provincial, though from a province, Spain, rich in grains and in human talent. He came to the imperial center, Rome, to get fame and fortune by his art of ridicule. He won the fame, at least, though he had at times to crawl for it–as did his fellow Spaniards Seneca, Lucan, and Quintilian. He crawled a bit more nimbly than they, since Nero arranged the deaths of Seneca and Lucan. Martial got to Rome just as Nero's reign was ending, but he had to live through a long reign of the repressive emperor Domitian (81–96 CE). He dodged and flattered well enough to get safely back to Spain, late in his fifties, where he praised his escape to primitive bliss–until he had to give up the pretense. He yearned back toward the city, cesspool though he called it. He had to have material for his satire.

He was like later gossip columnists, out night after night

prowling for what they can devour by denouncing. He is a Winchell in elegiac distichs. Or, more properly, he is like the gossip columnist in Evelyn Waugh's *Vile Bodies*, who makes a living off the absurdities and vices of his own society by mocking them. He is a complicitous critic, half enjoying what he sneers at, mixing entertainment with revulsion. He is a reforming voyeur, a compromised Savonarola. It is a complex role, not reducible to any one of its components.

What connection might Martial have with modern America? Well, like the Romans, we Americans celebrate rural virtue while wallowing in urban vices. Augustus, in founding the empire, pretended to be saving the republic. This set up an endless round of antinomies, of people professing simple pieties while indulging in complex depravities–the very people Martial homed in on with his radar for pretense and masquerading. Romans ostentatiously disavowed the depravity, real and supposed, of Greece, of "Oriental" cults and fads, while jostling each other to get at that forbidden fruit.

Of course, other cultures have felt the same stresses and rumblings, and I do Martial no service by comparing him with Winchell. Gossip columnists have come in much more artistic forms. A Swift, a Pope, a Dryden have played the court tattletale and raised their snide whisperings to a kind of cosmic thunder over the end of civilized behavior. Pope turned the heroic couplet into a literary guillotine. Head after head rolled away from his exquisite apparatus. Here goes Lord Hervey's noll:

> Fop at the toilet, flatterer at the board,
> Now trips a lady, and now struts a lord.

And here goes Addison's:

> Like Cato give his little Senate laws,
> And sit attentive to his own applause.

Or those of fading dowagers:

> A fop their passion, and their prize a sot;
> Alive ridiculous, and dead forgot.

And here he dispatches his critics:

> Yes, I am proud; I must be proud to see
> Men not afraid of God, afraid of me.

Martial, too, is a master of the quick dispatch (8.54):

> You're beautiful and sinful–in a trice
> I'd settle for less looks to get less vice.

Just as quick (11.66):

> How can the slippery son of a bitch,
> With all his vices, not be rich?

Or (12.20):

> Of course we know he'll never wed.
> What? Put his sister out of bed?

Or (2.38):

> What, Linus, can my farm be minus
> When it successfully lacks Linus?

Or (3.9):

> His verse was meant to strike me low,
> But since *he* wrote it–who will know?

Or (12.54):

> In you there's not a single thing to laud.
> To turn out honest were your greatest fraud.

Some translators of Martial feel that to be modern, to be authentic, they must not resort to things as forced, now, and artificial, as regular meter, stanzas, rhyme. But if that is how they feel, they should steer clear of ancient epigram, whose whole appeal lies in a studied formality. To have any force at all, epigram must add artifice to baser urges. In English we lack most of the resources of such artifice–the endlessly inter-lockable verbal patterns of an inflected language. We lack that form's verbal architectonics. If we give up tools that offer even

partial recompense for the loss of such structure, the En-
glished epigrams lose their focus. Martial was as focused as a
predator stalking its prey. His light but hard-hitting lines
blend low matter with high polish, the intimate and the im-
personal, the tough and the graceful. They pick up dung with
silver tongs.

The point of some epigrams is to get close enough in the
early lines to deliver a sudden stab in the last. Over and over
the tone can seem praising, luring the victim close enough for
a final vicious swerve to strike home (4.84):

> Men flock to Thais
>   From north and south,
> Yet she's a virgin—
>   All but her mouth.

The epigram toys with its victim, as cats play with mice
(4.87):

> Cold Bassa leans and coos
>   At baby's little shoes.
> Shows warmth of heart?
>   No, masks a fart.

But at other times, instead of wanting to get near enough for
intimate betrayal, the epigrammatist does not allow others to
get near him. A prize example comes from Catullus, who
wrote epigrams rarely but superbly—as in this response to an
overture from Julius Caesar (93):

Join your party?
  I might,
    mighty Czar,
Could I remember
  quite
    who you are.

That cool brush-off makes Samuel Johnson look clumsy and overheated when he spurns Lord Chesterfield's offer of patronage. The supreme statement of a haughty distance may be Martial 1.32:

Mister Sabidius, you pain me.
I wonder (some) why that should be
And cannot tell–a mystery.
You inexplicably pain me.

Catullus could fight dirty–not with brass knuckles, but golden knuckles (I6):

For veritable man I cannot pass?
Then what's that down your mouth and up your ass?
I thrust into the right receptacle–
For what you say is not acceptable.
You claim my verses seem effeminate
In what they hint and what they boldly state.
But poets are not what they write for others.
Their lives may meet the standard of their mothers.

> I write not for the young, combustible,
> Forever ready and all lust-able.
> I want to bring back ancients who were young–
> My lines reanimate the feebly hung.
> You think I've aged into the latter class?
> Then what's that down your mouth and up your ass?

Martial, too, could fight dirty (6.36):

> A bent huge nose, a monstrous cock to match,
> Curved each into the other, what a snatch!

The epigrammatists dignified such exercises by claiming disgust at social decline or aberration. They even claimed a noble lineage. As Homer founded epic, epigram had a legendary forebear in the seventh-century Greek poet Archilochus. As Horace put it in *The Poet's Craft* (79):

> Archilochus made anger keep its head,
> And killed men metronomically dead.

Of course, one could not openly rebuke an emperor in Martial's repressive era, when poets survived (if they did) by a studied (only slightly snickering) sycophancy. Like his friends and fellow Spaniards Seneca and Lucan, Martial tried to calculate the least degree of abasement he could get away with, alternately chafing at the boundaries and knuckling under. Under Domitian's reign (81–96), Martial could not venture even veiled subversion; but, like most of his contemporaries, he welcomed the brief respite under Nerva (96–98 CE), and earlier, with Titus (79–81 CE), he seemed genuinely enthusiastic. He wrote a series of little poems to celebrate that emperor's opening of his amphitheater (later called the Colosseum). Though it is a myth that Christians were fed to lions in that huge colander of blood, the combat of gladiators with each other and with beasts was sufficiently bloody, and Martial expresses a fan's delight in the mayhem. He was a Roman after all, and how can the author of epigrams question any art of cruelty? He admires the way a huge animal can be defeated with nothing more substantial than fisherman's gear (*Spectacles* 11):

> Rolled over in the bloody dust,
> The bear can make no freeing thrust.
> The thin compulsion of a net
> Is firm in gauzy layers set.
> So beasts can, though they soar in air,
> Come netted earthward, like the bear.

For Martial, the epigrammatist was a *retiarius*. He at least half-meant his abject praise of Titus as Master of the Games (*Spectacles* 31):

> My hurried style no criticism raises–
> One never errs in hurrying your praises.

Despite such kowtowing to the forms of patronage, Martial likes to undermine most forms of convention. Ancient poets liked

Catullus' picture of a girl lamenting her pet bird, a sentimental scene from Greuze. Martial will seem to indulge the same device, only to reveal its sexual subtheme in one line (7.14):

> Fate humbles her, she's lost her pet,
>     No bird by soft Catullus sung,
> No dove plunged to a hell of jet,
>     Whose praises stretch the poet's lung.
> Rather, a mite of few years yet,
>     But mightily already hung.

Everything in Martial's short insult poems exists for the final thrust. We are meant to respond as the Venetian friar did when stabbed by Vatican henchmen: "I get the point" (*stilo*). English translations sacrifice other things to get to the essential. This often makes the translation more economical than its original, since Martial's preliminary fencing is done with tools we cannot use.

Martial belonged to the educated class that, in the Roman Empire, could live by patronage and art, so long as one did not challenge the established system (as Ovid and Lucan did). There was little danger of that with Martial, since he was a social conservative, as are most satirists who castigate "deviants" (Juvenal and Persius in the ancient world, Pope and Waugh later on). Martial seems "daring" because he pushes conventional limits, but he does it for conventional standards. His poems are bisexual in the accepted way of his time, praising pliable boys and frisky women, but he upholds classical misogyny and the view that the only decent homosexual relation is that of an active male adult and a passive boy. Other relationships, including any between women and women, are treated as shameful—as are all forms of oral sex (fellatio as well as cunnilingus, whether performed by males or females).

For Martial, the highest virtue is friendship, and the greatest wrong is betrayal of friends. His frequent attacks on the patronage system (by which he lived) focus on the way most patrons failed to rise to the level of friendship professed by them. Treating men of power as friends keeps him from thinking he has to accept their political programs. The deepest statement of his values may be this (5.42):

> A thief can rifle any till,
> A fire with ash your home can fill,
> A creditor calls in your debt.
> Bad harvest does your farm upset,
> An impish mistress robs your dwelling,
> Storm shatters ships with water swelling.
> But gifts to friends your friendships save.
> You keep thus always what you gave.

He dwells often on the complex etiquette of gift-giving and gift-receiving, loans extended and loans unpaid, banquets welcoming or dismissing clients. The epigrams are a treasure trove of information on the Roman social customs of his time. Martial celebrates his and his friends' birthdays. (He was named Martialis for his own birth in March, the month of Mars.) His misogyny did not prevent him from accepting a villa in his native Spain from a female patron, and his apolitical life did not keep him from sycophancy to the emperors. The greatest moralists know how to cut moral corners. We like them still when they attack the *other* hypocrites in their world.

Not all of Martial's epigrams are satirical or insulting. He often pays tribute–to a friend, a hero, a landscape. One of the heroes he celebrates is the Younger Cato's daughter, Portia (1.42):

> Of Brutus' end when frantic Portia learned,
> Her friends hid weapons while for death she yearned.
> She cried, "Who keeps me from my chosen date?
> Like Cato's daughter I shall earn my fate."
> Deprived of arms, she took coals from the fire
> And, swallowing death, achieved her last desire.
> Vainly to keep her from the sword they tried–
> Some forms of steel are not to be denied.

He could pay a friend this gracious compliment (1.39):

> If ancient virtues could abound,
> If wisdom were with goodness found,
> If learning did with vigor thrive,
> And loyalty were still alive,
> If challenged honor were defended,
> And gods were not by stealth offended,
> If any of these things were true–
> Where find them, Decius, but in you?

To avoid crass flattery, he can turn a wry compliment (12.51):

> Friend Gullible, so often taken in,
> Lacks our familiarity with sin.

He could be tender, as in this lament for a little slave (5.34):

> My parents in the Underworld! I send
> This servant girl–take care and gently tend,
> Conduct her past the terrifying shade.
> Keep her of circling horrors unafraid,
> For she, alas, was only six days shy
> Of six years when too soon she came to die.
> Protect her as she plays her childhood games,
> And lisps, as shyly she was wont, our names.
> Earth, sadly mounded on this gravesite new,
> Press lightly on her, as she did on you.

The only tender love poems are pederastic, like this (10.42):

> Your hint of beard just barely is,
> It is a froth, a breath, a fizz.
> A sunbeam or a wandering breeze
> Displaces it with nudging ease.
> Girls brush it with a dainty thumb
> That sweeps the down off from a plum.
> And when you give me kisses free,
> Your shadow beard dusts off on me.

The classical view of pederasty was the opposite of ours. We accept gay sex between consenting adults, but treat sex with minors as child abuse. But the latter was the ideal for moralists of Martial's time.

Martial sometimes poses as a henpecked husband, but only because that is a typical comic situation. He never married. When the emperor Titus gave him "the privilege of three children" (*jus trium liberorum*)–an incentive Augustus instituted to increase the population–it was a reward for Martial's poem on the opening of the amphitheater. Martial had no children, at least not legitimate ones.

But for all his softer or more lyrical epigrams, Martial will always be best known for his insult poems, the dirtier the better. He often attacks promiscuity, here with a typical twist at the end (7.30):

> Barbarian hordes en masse you fuck,
> Odd types into your bed you tuck,
> You take on blacks and Asian forces,
> And Jews, and soldiers, and their horses.
> Yet you, voracious Roman chick,
> Have never known a Roman dick.

Here is the insult parliamentary (6.23):

> You want my cock at full attention
> If sex you casually mention?
> No matter how you coax men's tools,
> Hand "makes a motion" face o'errules.

And this is the insult histrionic (6.6):

> Your lady's with the art scene all aglow.
> To theater she is devoted so,
> That, after screwing each star in the show,
> To players of the "smallest parts" she'll go.

Here is as far as insult can go (7.18):

> Your face entices, and your thighs–
> Why are you shunned by all the guys?
> Because when in your cunt they drill,
> Its liquids clack and gurgle, shrill.
> You hold your tongue–no other part
> Will sound off (not a single fart).
> But cunt keeps up its squish and squeal
> Of gibberish without repeal.
> You hope your men will cease to balk?
> Then teach that lower mouth to talk.

But for all the interesting matter in these epigrams, it is their manner that Martial was really interested in, the way he played his verbal games. The most striking feature of his poems is their self-referentiality. In the index of subjects at the end of this book, it is apparent that Martial's main subject was the writer's life–his own work, his models, his audience, his rivals, his patrons. That it was all a game can be seen from the fact that he boasts that he never harmed a living reputation. (Pope would have considered himself a failure if that had been said of him.) Martial referred to real people, and used their real names, in his praise poems. He does not direct his attack poems against real people (unlike Dryden and Pope), and the names he uses are fictitious (not pseudonyms, as in Pope). The names are there to give a spurious particularity to the game, along with sonorous sound effects. Often they are Greek names, to appeal to the Roman suspicion of "Eastern" perversions. Since such names do not fit as readily into English iambs as they do into Latin elegiacs—and since they are not real names, and they have not the sinister Greek aura to the modern reader—I omit most proper names in the attack poems. It is often said that epigrams should be sampled one or a few at a time. Martial thought so, too. He wrote (10.1):

> If this book seems too long,
> Just read from it one song.
> In this way, whittling it
> And reading bit by bit,
> A little book with ease
> You make it, as you please.

The way Martial played his game *as a game* can be seen in his inventive creation of outlandish hyperbole, as at 11.21, which has the absurdist fantasy of an obscene Edward Lear:

> Her cunt—broad as an asshole that you
> Might spot on some equestrian statue—
> Is wide as rolling hoop that thumps you,
> Wide as the wheel a gymnast jumps through,

As gaping as a rotten shoe
Or thrown net that the light shines through,
As wambly as an unfurled awning,
Or bracelet from a thin arm yawning,
As floppy as an emptied pillow,
Or lax as hobo pants that billow,
As gulping as a pelican
That fish into its pouch does cram.
They claim I fucked her in a pond?
Not so, since her cunt *is* the pond!

That is not a malicious attack on some real woman, but a naughty game meant to elicit a socially pretentious shock. The effect he aimed for is clear from 6.60:

He reads my verses, just to be in fashion,
But finds himself whipsawed by sudden passion.
He frowns, then chortles–chokes at what he reads–
And calls them the most infamous of screeds,
Then he goes pale, as under some indicting–
You've got him, poems! That's what I call writing.

–Garry Wills

# MARTIAL'S EPIGRAMS

# BOOK ONE

## Introduction

TO THE CRITIC

You knew the play was of a naughty kind,
No subject for a puritan's closed mind—
Why join us in the theater at all?
To signal scorn by rushing from your stall?

### 1.1

Your cravings I no longer can deny:
This is the little book for which you cry,
All slyly made of literary taunts
To demonstrate that nothing Martial daunts
And merit honor for my living verse
That men departed get for poems worse.

## 1.3

### TO HIS BOOK ON BEING PUBLISHED

Why, little book, steal from my shelf
To shift in danger for yourself
In all the low dives of the city?
You will be hooted without pity,
The very babes will join the snub,
Turn tiny rhino noses up.
You'll be one moment taking bows,
Then pummeled more than law allows.
For this you left my pen corrective,
Still working on your lines defective?
You'd rather lurk and dodge through Rome
Than keep your honor here at home?

## 1.4

### TO THE EMPEROR

If you should ever stumble on my book,
Briefly put off your world-compelling look,
Remember, rulers have let insults fly
At triumphs, to defeat the evil eye.
You fancy risqué mimes upon the stage—
So let a lowly author stain his page.
A censor can relax, wink just one eye:
My poetry is filthy—but not I.

## 1.8

### AGAINST CATO

If, unlike Cato, you stay pure,
Forgoing suicide's allure,
I find you better for denying
Cheap praise solicited by dying.

## 1.9

High virtue you would join with social climbing,
But climbers must for virtue end repining.

## 1.10

Wooing, he pushes gifts on her,
Would wed, permitting no demur.
To beauty she has no presumption.
What makes her so desired? Consumption.

## 1.11

All water you invariably decline–
Where others water wine, you wine your wine.

## 1.13

### ARRIA'S SWORD

She said, "This hurt not when it ran me through,"
And gave it him: "I die when it kills you."

1.16

Some good things here, and some not worth a look.
For this is that anomaly, a book.


1.17

"In law you could be great,
    All foes disarming."
But I prefer a safer state,
    My greatness? Farming.


1.18

Why sully your well-mellowed wines
With acid pressings from raw vines?
Did trusted vintages offend?
What presents did the new stuff send?
Each crime or merit you exceed
By mingling noble with low breed.
Your *guests* may merit poison, true.
But murder not old *wine* with new.


1.19

Four teeth made up your total set.
You coughed out two, and had two yet.
Another cough was all it needed
To leave you with bare gums receded.
Now you are blessed–for endless coughing
Leaves nothing in your mouth for offing.

I.20

While guests looked at the marvel, as in fable,
You bolted down each mushroom on the table.
What fitting recompense can now be forged
For all the monstrous feast that you engorged?
One provender alone is fit for you–
The mushroom that our emperor, Claudius, slew.

I.22

Why, rabbit, do you fear the lion's maw?
You were not made to dignify that jaw.
Not yours the sinews such teeth tear
Nor veins that noble bloodlines bear.
You're barely worth a puppy's glances.
Can toddlers face an army's lances?

I.23

No guest you beckon to your house's paths
But those encountered at the public baths;
Why I was never asked at last I knew–
I was no hearty of the bathing crew,
Where men without their clothes you could review.

I.24

Gruff with authentic virtue, he
Affects the true nobility.
Well has he purchased social pride:
He is a highborn noble's–bride.

### 1.25

Your modest ways now firmly set aside,
No longer literary talent hide.
For you can write what tasteful Greeks would praise
And critics honor even in our days.
Why fight off fame now beating at your door?
What other writers dare to promise more?
You must make immortality start now,
Not make it wait to give your corpse a bow.

### 1.27

When drinks I had beyond my number,
I thought I would myself encumber
With pledge to give you lunch today.
You wrote it down with great display
As if to register disputed votes.
I hate a tippler taking notes.

### 1.28

They claimed, with blamings not condign,
He reeked at morn of last night's wine.
He intermits not in such ways:
Not last night's wine—it was today's.

### 1.30

As doctor, both, and undertaker,
He took men off to meet their maker.

1.32

Mister Sabidius, you pain me.
I wonder (some) why that should be
And cannot tell–a mystery.
You inexplicably pain me.


1.33

When Janet is sequestered, out of view,
    Then never for her father's death she cries.
But let some viewers come, just one or two,
    Then tears dramatically flood her eyes.
We know from this how sad in fact she's been:
It is not grief that's only grieved when seen.


1.34

Covert affairs give you no satisfaction.
For you, an unseen sin has no attraction.
From whores professional take you some tips,
Who serve their johns in darkness, with sealed lips.
If, outdoors, an unwanted viewer looms,
They'll even turn a trick behind some tombs.
Don't think me puritanical and mean:
I don't forbid the sin, just being seen.

1.35

My poetry is not what children read,
Or what their teachers try to make them heed.
But purer poems will make my readers sick
As any wife whose husband has no dick.
Since wedding poems bedward gaily go,
And festivals delight in naughty show,
There is some scope allowed for celebrating,
To keep us all in proper season mating.
So castrate not my ithyphallic verses.
Eunuchs are those who like to ride in hearses.
And who will ever see without a shock
A tame Priapus gelded of his cock?

1.36

Castor and Pollux could not put to shame
These brothers, worthy of a higher fame.
For Leda's sons rotated life and death,
Each taking turns to draw reviving breath.
These men would not their lives in segments give,
For each would tell the other, "Always live."

1.37

Your chamber pot is gold, your dish of glass—
You spend less on your mouth than on your ass.

1.38

Although the lines are mine (their worth assures)—
By badly singing them, you make them yours.

### 1.39

If ancient virtues could abound,
If wisdom were with goodness found,
If learning did with vigor thrive,
And loyalty were still alive,
If challenged honor were defended,
And gods were not by stealth offended,
If any of these things were true–
Where find them, Decius, but in you?

### 1.40

You castigate my poems,
   Every one.
May everything displease you,
   You please none.

### 1.42

Of Brutus' end when frantic Portia learned,
Her friends hid weapons while for death she yearned.
She cried, "Who keeps me from my chosen date?
Like Cato's daughter I shall earn my fate."
Deprived of arms, she took coals from the fire
And, swallowing death, achieved her last desire.
Vainly to keep her from the sword they tried–
Some forms of steel are not to be denied.

1.43

We left Bob's dinner hungrier than before.
A scrawny pig was served, and nothing more–
No grapes that sweeten slowly on the vine,
No apples honeyed rich as vintage wine,
No pears that flirt out from the twigs that hold them,
No fruits so deeply red that roses scold them.
The cheeses from the countryside stayed there.
The olive vessels stood of contents bare.
A pig we got! A dish to make us fidget,
A pig that could be strangled by a midget.
A pig less apt for eating than for viewing,
As in the Colosseum for hallooing
Game boars run by our empty abdomens
And writhe there, clawed, as bloody odds and ends.
Let such a pig be sent Bob by his friends.

1.44

You say my poems once or twice repeat
Things like the hare the lion would not eat.
Say, Stella, when you bid me dine with you,
Do you repeat a recipe or two?

1.46

"Orgasm!" you cry. "Now or never!"
A cry that detumesces ever.
If you would shape me for attack
Hurry me on by holding me back.

1.50

You call your cook "The High," to make men stare.
"–And Mighty" I'll call mine, to form a pair.

1.53

You slipped your poem into mine.
Which one is easy to divine–
Like one rag in a fashion show,
Or wood spoon in a silver row,
Like blackbird where the white swans gleam,
Or crow that nightingale would seem,
Your poem here does not belong.
My books authenticate by song.
Your work requires no outer brand.
The lines themselves shout, "Secondhand!"

1.54

Your life is crowded with old friends,
But room for new ones never ends.
Do you reject a friend that's new?
Your oldest friend was once that too.
The point is not the present state,
But where one finally will rate,
Time having put him to the test,
To rank as "old friend" with the rest.

### 1.55

You, first in war and politics,
Are stunned that I yearn for the sticks,
Not for a large farm, but my own,
Where modest needs are clearly known.
Why hope for halls that echo loud
With sycophants thronged in a crowd,
When netted game and angled fish
I'll crowd upon my humble dish,
When all my gold is sweetest honey,
And farmhands work for little money,
Their women serving fresh-laid eggs
On furniture with rough-hewn legs?
Should this my vision not seem pretty,
Then stay behind, pent in the city,
Stay pasty-faced and dull, not witty.

### 1.56

The rain pounds endless on and through your vines—
It's water you'll be selling us, not wines.

### 1.57

You ask what kind of girl I fancy—
One not too tame or one too chancy,
So bring me, to command my heart,
No coolest nun or hottest tart.

1.58

The boy cost more than I could pay,
So moneyed Tom took him away,
Which left me with complaining cock,
While Tom was setting me on mock.
But he had only done so well
By putting up his cock to sell.
Give me the cash, without such trade
A higher offer I'd have made.


1.60

Why, rabbit, flit into the lion's jaw,
Who does not notice you beneath his paw?
His mouth is framed for greater haunches' rending,
Not for a small thing's even smaller ending–
Not for catastrophe so risible,
Inhaled into his maw scarce visible.
For monstrous game, more worthy of his jowls,
He deadly through the darkest forest prowls.


1.62

She traveled far and near, a faithful wife,
Had never been reproached in all her life.
Rome found her chaster than the Sabines' story,
And Berlin added volumes to her glory.
But after Paris, she could boast no more.
She entered there a nun, came out a whore.

### 1.64

Of debutantes you are beyond compare–
So wealthy, beautiful, and debonair.
Yet you make all this matter not a whit:
Your beauty to undo–you boast of it.

### 1.65

#### TO A PEDANT

"Peestockyou nuts," I said–you laughed at me.
"*Pistashyos*–now pronounce it properly!"
Alright, I'll use Pistashyos for the nut–
"Pesstockyos" call the hemorrhoids on your butt.

### 1.66

You wish to be reputed as an author.
For others' stolen lines you make a proffer.
But why take *famous* words when you will show them
To connoisseurs who have the sense to know them?
You need to find some raw unpublished works,
Not yet refined or purged of all their quirks.
My own drafts I hide deep as secret thought–
Silence cannot be plagiarized or bought.

### 1.67

I grant you there is foul stuff in my book.
But why? You're in it–take a look.

1.68

Jack thinks or speaks of nothing but his Jill,
He gets of fantasizing her no fill.
If Jill should be entirely made away,
He'd stranded be, with nothing left to say.
Why even when he states accounts to dad,
He says it is to Jill his debts are had.
Jill shyly laughs, but not her jealous mate.
Tell him, "There's more than one Jill in the state."

1.69

Pan's statue once seemed comic as a pup–
Now they show *you*, which cracks them up.

1.71

In naming with each toast my favorite lasses,
I match the letters in their name with glasses.
So Laevia takes six, Justina seven,
Lyde takes four, and Ida three, and heaven
'Twould be exhausting all the alphabet,
But Stupor overtakes me before that.

1.72

Because you use my quips around the town,
You think you've nailed your reputation down.
As well should toothless Ann her dentures boast,
Or black Jill think her white who powders most.
A wig hides no bald pate for those who know it–
Nor will my pilfered lines make you a poet.

### 1.73

To screw your wife, unguarded, no one cared.
But once you barred her door, a thousand dared.

### 1.74

#### WED TO A SCOUNDREL

You screwed a man in whom you took no pride.
How, then, your shame (who's now your husband) hide?

### 1.77

Healthy enough, Charles yet is pale,
His drinks do tell no red-flushed tale,
He pants, but palely, should he run,
And tans not in the hottest sun.
Cosmetics cannot make him ruddier–
At last we learn why, with a shudder.
No blood into his cheeks will rush,
Since he licks cunt, and does not blush.

1.85

The auctioneer praised all the land
Its solvent owner had in hand.
The man was not in need of gold,
His purse had all that it could hold.
Why sell, then? Well, the slaves all fled,
The crops were withered, flocks were dead.
It takes no fiscal skill to tell
This land no realtor will sell
If he should live a million lives.
Why purchase land where nothing thrives?

1.86

### THE CELEBRITY

I can from my house reach a hand
And touch where Henry's house does stand.
I'm told how lucky I must be
Where I can Henry always see.
But I could just as well reside
Upon some distant mountainside
For all the chance I have to meet
This nearby Absence on my street.
You must be near him—almost be him—
To be assured you'll never see him.

1.87

### THE SOUSE

The reek of last night's wine you'd slacken
With breath mints that your dentures blacken.
The reek is back when once you vent
The rumblings from your innards sent.
In fact the mints give staying power
To make your stench last by the hour.
Your last night's drinks you will disclose,
Identified by every nose.

1.90

I never saw you, Bassa, with a man.
No rumor ever spread of an affair.
You seemed as chaste as any woman can,
With Lucrece pure you made a worthy pair.
Belatedly I found I venerated,
A woman who a woman penetrated.
You found an amphisbaenic instrument–
To give cunts simultaneous content.
You pose a riddle Sphinxes never knew,
To be a woman and a woman screw.

1.91

### THE CRITIC

With carpings you my works revile,
    Your own you never publish.
Without such works, your carpings I'll
    Consider snooty rubbish.


1.110

You say I write lines longer than I ought?
It's true your lines are shorter–they are nought.


1.118

He who can read a hundred quips in verse
Would flinch not at a thousand ordeals worse.

# BOOK TWO

### 2.1

Well, book, you could be bulkier, by far.
But who would really want more than you are?
Your pride is that less paper is consumed,
Which means that less of scandal was exhumed.
To copy you is not a tedious task,
And reading you is not too much to ask–
Who opens you while cocktails first are taken
Can end before another round is shaken.
But even so some will believe you wrong.
Some think that reading anything's too long.

### 2.3

Indebtedness of yours will never mount,
Since debts one will not (cannot) pay–don't count.

2.4

Your mother calls you, "Brother," cooing,
You answer her with crawly wooing.
You her too sisterly affection
Reciprocate without rejection—
With deary son and sweetie mother,
There's hanky-panky, each to other.


2.5

It is a special treat to visit you,
There are few things that I would rather do.
The two miles there are pleasant at the start,
But travel two miles back can test the heart.
For often when I get there you are gone,
Or wrapped in your own business from the dawn,
And though you wish me well, you will not see me,
Or from my disappointment ever free me.
I see you after two miles and feel rich,
But four miles *not* to see you is a bitch.

2.6

You always want from me a book that's new,
Yet this one you have never read clear through.
The time was, you would memorize my lines
And showily recite them at all times.
Do my lines some new inspiration need?
No, you are just too lazy, now, to read.
You're one who plans for mighty expeditions
With maps and tour guides of the last editions,
Provision takes by emptying the cupboard,
Yet does not get entirely to—the suburb.
And so you wish I would provision you—
You always want from me a book that's new.

2.7

At oratory you're not bad,
Your legal fees make no one sad,
At turning verses you will pass,
And singing on key to a lass.
All things you do so nearly well,
It all adds up to—bloody hell.

2.8

Say what I write is problematical,
Obscure, obtuse, or not grammatical–
Why blame that on the writer, not the scribe?
He dropped a line, the fault of all his tribe.
But you persist in making me at fault,
A matter of most personal assault.
Convict my stuff, and damn it by the letter–
However bad, you never could do better.

2.9

I wrote for her–she would not come away.
I'm done for, so would many people say.
She opened it and reads? I'll get my way.

2.12

Of foreign realms exotic, spicy-rare,
You waft the most expensive-fragrant air.
When always you exude new odors dishy,
Beneath the perfume something's fishy.

2.13

Why bribe a judge to hedge your bets
When you could simply pay the debts?

2.15

That you pass not your cup, sick heiress,
Is *not* rude, but a way to spare us.

### 2.20

A poet's name is what you sought.
The name, you found, is all you bought.

### 2.21

Offered his handshake or his kiss,
Be sure the latter course to miss.

### 2.25

You always lie when saying you'll accept me.
Keep lying, promise that you will reject me.

### 2.26

She exercises on you all her feeble charm.
You foolishly are taking no alarm.
You hope hers is a nearly-fatal cough?
She's coughing you "Come on," not going off.

### 2.28

They slander you who call you fucked or fucker.
You do not for such action ever pucker.
Nor penetrating and nor penetrated?
What acts are left need not, we know, be stated.

### 2.33

You think that I will kiss your head—
So bald and polished, one-eyed, red?
That were an upside-downside trick,
To kiss, up there, a cranial dick.

2.38

What, Linus, can my farm be minus
When it successfully lacks Linus?

2.42

Dip your bum in the bathing place!
Don't stain it deeper—with your face.

2.43

We know what your wife thinks of you, her man.
From how she chose your gelded guardian.

2.49

Make her my wife? But only if she toys
With specially delicious sexy boys.
If screwing in her bed I catch the two,
As husband, legally, I can him screw.

2.50

No wonder that you suck, then take the cup.
That's just the place that needs some cleaning up.

2.51

It's late, you're down to your last cash,
A coin that's worn smooth as your ass.
It won't on food or drink be spent,
But on the biggest dick for rent.
Your stomach has a fainting spell
From watching how your ass does well.

### 2.52

Her breasts unwieldy so obstruct her path,
She buys two extra tickets at the bath.

### 2.55

You want to be my patron and my friend.
If you insist on patron, good-bye friend!

### 2.56

**THE AMBASSADOR'S WIFE**

You do your foreign service. So does she.
But she imposes no colonial fee.
No, she—to any who will take her—free
Extends her "diplomatic courtesy."

### 2.60

You screw a warlike captain's wife
And have no worry for your life.
If caught, you think, he'll only rape you—
But may, in harsher fact, castrate you.
"Has he for justice little awe?"
Does what *you're* doing meet the law?

### 2.61

Your fresh boy's face, so sweet to see,
Pumped grown-ups' cocks ferociously.
Now your sour face, too grim to bury,
Enough to make the hangman chary,
Is used to curse and blight the land,
Heaps insults more than one can stand.
Return that tongue to nobler use,
Sucking is purer than abuse.

### 2.62

Your pubic hair you trim to please your lass.
For whom do you so neatly groom your ass?

### 2.64

The courts, or lecture hall? You can't decide,
But, hesitant, you cast your life aside.
You diddle more than Nestor's years away
And will not posthumously get your say.
Now three top lecturers are taken off,
You could be elocution's reigning toff.
Or if law cases you desire to plead,
The very courthouse statues will take heed.
Your years are not indefinitely loant.
By stalling over what you'll be, you won't.

2.65

Troubled you appear today?
"I am, my wife's just passed away."
And all her riches you inherit?
I'd say your troubles have some merit.


2.66

A lock of her well-pampered hair flopped free.
Her glass made her this horrid error see.
Against her hairdresser she smashed the glass,
Her baldness should for smoothest mirror pass!


2.67

So many hours you ask men, "How d'you do?"
There is no energy for more with you.


2.71

When I recite one of my poems past,
You bring up other poets who will last.
Is this comparison to make me shine?
You'd do that best if you recited thine.


2.73

When drunk, she can't remember what she did?
Same as when sober–sucks dick at first bid.

2.76

Ample he left you in his will,
You gave him nothing. Who's the shill?

2.77

You say my epigrams run on too long.
You want to set a limit to my song.
For you the Colosseum is too high,
And figurines too tiny for the eye.
Against vice Pope did lengthily inveigh,
Yet every line would accurately weigh.
Proportion calls for calibrated touch.
From you a *single* line is far too much.

2.80

He killed himself, lest from the foe he'd fly.
What logic's here?—Rather than die, to die?

2.82

To hide your heinous crime,
    Your slave's tongue you cut out.
Therefore that act of thine
    The whole world now will shout.

2.83

The man gave you the cuckold's horn?
His ears and nose your knife has shorn.
Have you deprived him of a screw?
Just ask his mouth what it can do.

2.84

The one who slaughtered Venus' favored one,
She punished with hard drudgings in his bum.
The one who killed her son must bear the brunt
With endless dark obsession to lick cunt.


2.86

I write no labyrinthine verse
That fags affectedly rehearse,
Avant-garde poetry exotic
Appealing to this week's neurotic.
What would you have my verselets do,
Put boxers in a pink tutu?
To earn a natural esteem,
Light things should not pretentious seem.
Let pedants cultivate their clique.
My poems more directly speak.


2.89

You grant you drink—just look at Cato's nose.
Your poems stink—but so did Cicero's.
Like Antony you cannot hold your liquor,
Apricius spent too much? You do it quicker.
For every fault you have a model pat.
But sucking dick? What great forebear did that?

# BOOK THREE

### 3.8

She lacks an eye—who'll love her true?
If Quintus does, then he lacks two.

### 3.9

His verse was meant to strike me low,
But since *he* wrote it—who will know?

### 3.15

Nobody is more trusting, credit-wise:
He's doubly blind, in love and in the eyes.

### 3.17

Dessert was passed from hand to hand,
And no one could its heat withstand,
But Sabby blew on it with mighty force,
Cooled it in ways all could endorse.
But each in turn, disgusted, threw it.
Its fatal taint was that he blew it.

### 3.18

Performer has a cold tonight?
Then spare us all—and don't recite!

### 3.26

You own a famous and a vast estate,
With precious jewels, silver, and gold plate.
You stock your cellars with the choicest wine,
And treasure wisdom that's almost divine.
There's only one thing that you lack in life.
You lack possession of one thing—your wife.

### 3.27

Invited, you invite not back.
Yet my devoirs you never lack.
So this will be the sum of all:
I am all guiled, and you all gall.

### 3.28

Why should his ear so smell of shit?
Because you whispered into it.

### 3.32

No, woman, *not* screw you—because you're old?
Yes, I've a problem when a corpse turns cold.
Old Hecuba I'd tupped before she changed—
Gods metamorphosed her to a dog deranged.
I might have got it on with Niobe
Before a landmark weeping-stone was she.

3·33

I want a non-slave woman for my bed,
Or slave to freedom now delivered.
But find a slave more pretty than those two—
Well, faute de mieux, I'll find room for her too.

3·34

"Snowy," your name is partly right,
For you are cold—but hardly white.

3·35

Fish carved so true and trim
That, watered, they will swim.

3·40

This lizard, carved, delights the sight,
But touch it not—for it might bite.

3·42

You use a cream your wrinkles to disguise,
But you're just pulling wool over our eyes.
The wrinkles, left alone, would draw no mention,
But, covered up, they draw closest attention.

3.44

You wonder why no people pay you heed?
Well, I'll unveil the mystery—you read.
Incessantly you foist on us your rhymes,
A legendary peril of our times.
No mother tiger snarling near her cubs,
No snake attacking us despite our clubs,
No scorpion paralyzingly come near,
Can deal us such humiliating fear
As you, in undeterr'd reciting mode
Producing endless drivel by the load.
I stop and you are dinning in my ear,
I run and hear you panting in the rear.
You fill our homes with unremitting roar.
I even hear you through the outhouse door.
A public nuisance at the public bathing,
For tow'ls you give us pages for our swathing.
To dinner we go in, out comes your verse,
The same old tired nonsenses, or worse.
At street corners we timorously look
To see if you are lurking in a nook,
Poised to bombard us with your lethal book.
I go to bed and still I hear you drone,
Have you no soundproof hovel of your own?
Some honesty you have, but far below it,
You are that deepest pestilence—a poet.

3.45

Why did the Sun flee from Thyestes' dinner?
Though I'm not sure, your feast could be the winner,
Not by providing more exotic treats
Than any but the nicest palate eats.
Would you provide us with our favorite dish?
Just stop reciting–that's our fondest wish.


3.49

Your cup breathes odors fine
That never come from mine.
Better is what you waft
Than what I'm forced to quaff.


3.51

I praise your face and figure as divine.
"But if you saw me nude–I really shine."
Yet rather than shed clothes you seek distraction.
Because a letdown will be my reaction?


3.52

Your new house was by fire ended.
But contributions you befriended.
The fire five times its worth arouses.
You could grow rich by burning houses.

### 3.53

I would not miss your face or lips
Or anything around your hips.
Why itemize the whole list through?
The truth is—I will not miss you.

### 3.54

Why set for sex a price I cannot pay?
Be still more forthright, just send me away.

### 3.55

You walk in swirls of spicy air,
Spread rich aromas everywhere.
But do not play us for a dummy.
With perfume on, my dog smells yummy.

### 3.57

Ravenna's not of water springs the nurse,
And therefore I was cheated in reverse.
For when I thought to drink wine as I dined, it
Proved that he watered not my wine, but wined it.

### 3.61

Since "only a mere nothing" you request.
You'll get it—for that nothing, be my guest.

### 3.64

The Sirens with hypnotic sensuous singing,
Their joyous ecstasies and sweet death bringing,
No man, they used to boast, could ever leave them,
Till sly Ulysses did at last deceive them.
But easier their enchantments to disperse
Than stopping Canius' story in mid-verse.

### 3.65

The misty smell of apples bitten,
Or senses with new spices smitten,
The wafture from a ripening vine,
Cropped grasses like a subtle wine,
The odor of the richest myrrh,
Brought by Arabian laborer,
Rubbed amber, incense in the fire,
Rain rippling like melodic lyre,
A garland mixing its perfume
With soft hairs woven like a loom—
All these lie in this boy's caress.
Then why not give of his largesse?

3.66

Pothinus matched Mark Antony in crime.
They slew the noblest Romans of their time.
The august victims they decapitated,
An act of infamy with shame related.
One head was Pompey's who brought triumphs home.
The other Cicero's, the voice of Rome.
Pothinus acted for another man, on hire.
Mark Antony indulged his own desire.

3.68

I warn you, ladies, read not what's to come,
It's made of naughty stuff to strike you dumb.
No more polite lines I reserve for you.
It's time for me to serve my own tastes too.
We're going to the men's baths, to strip bare.
No woman claiming morals can be there.
To keep the reputation of your race,
You must, with careful hands before your face,
Avoid Priapus coming into view
(With fingers loose enough for seeing through)—
I know that boredom made you doubt my art,
But now you'll pant long at every part.

### 3.69

To purer lines than yours none can aspire–
Morality in verse could not mount higher.
I write, I must confess, for dirtier readers,
My verse does not attract the nation's leaders.
For earthy company I sing things new.
The chaster (fewer) sort I leave to you.

### 3.70

Your present mistress once you held as wife,
With whom you could not live a wedded life.
Unless provoked by sexual transgression,
You obviously can't achieve erection.

### 3.71

The boy has got the active penis,
And you an ass smooth as a Venus.
I need therefore no hidden clue
To figure out just what you do.

### 3.72

You pant for me both night and day
But won't your naked charms display.
Because you have a flabby breast,
A cunt as vile as buzzard's nest?
The real truth, which you can't contain,
Is simply that you have no brain.

### 3.73

Your boy's the one that has the hard-on
While your poor prick must ask for pardon.
I thought 'twas you that played the man
But find receive is all you can.

### 3.78

Again piss to the windward, mate?
That makes you palin-urinate.

### 3.80

You libel none in glee,
   Nor slander round the 'hood.
Then why do all agree,
   Your tongue's up to no good?

### 3.81

O who could find a eunuch priest in you?
One end of you can serve no woman, true,
But if you would in truth be found unmated,
Your tongue, not cock, must be castrated.

### 3.82

His entertainment is like brothel-goods.
He gives to favorites the finest foods.
The rest of us get fed with various scraps.
He even thinks we'll stay while he takes naps.
And yet at him we do not rail or scoff.
And why is that? Because he sucks us off.

3.87

At baths, you cover your parts south,
   Which have not known a dick.
But why not cover up your mouth,
   The place wherein you lick.


3.88

The problem of these twins still vexes.
They go down, but on different sexes.
It makes for a distinction nice–
Are they identical in vice?


3.89

Try some emollients finely grated–
Your face makes you look constipated.


3.90

No she says first, and then says yes.
What *does* she want? No one can guess.


3.100

I sent this book despite the rain.
The courier guarded it from stain.
Did it get wet when moved about?
All right–it needed washing out.

# BOOK FOUR

4.5

What makes you qualified to come to Rome?
What poor and virtuous man can call it home?
Are you a pimp, a social butterfly,
Do you drag men into the court to die?
Not you, you do not take a close friend's wife,
Or screw old women as they end their life,
Or play in politics the cringing hack,
Or rally to some new performer's claque.
With all these disadvantages, why think
You'd flourish in this cesspool stink?
"I have a friend worth trusting all the time."
With that, you'll never make a single dime.

### 4.13

My dear friend takes a wife, and we must light
The marriage torches that will bless this night.
As sweet is joined with spicy, or as wine
Is soothed with honey, or as curling vine
Does climb and hang as close as close can be
Around the trunk of its protective tree,
As waterlily floats in liquid rest,
Or rooted myrtle shines onshore its best—
So be they harmonized in wedded life.
Let Venus bless them both and ease all strife.
When they grow old, let her his ills assuage;
Let him not even recognize her age.

### 4.18

The water dripping from the gate
Took on a pointy frozen state,
And as a boy was passing under,
It fell and stabbed him like ice-thunder.
Fortune will find new ways to trick us.
We learn that it can water-drip us.

### 4.20

Cute Alice claims that she's a hag;
Old Judy's youth-pose makes one gag.
Our view we cannot hide or scarf—
One makes us laugh, one makes us barf.

### 4.21

This darkling world he claims, with rue,
   Has run itself into a ditch.
And he can prove his thesis true:
   In such a cosmos—he is rich.

### 4.22

The bride too shy to yield to her first lover,
Plunged into crystal waters as a cover,
But her bright-twinkling limbs kept shining through
As lilies in a vase, still clear to view,
And all her dazzling beauty, as it chanced,
Erotically moistened, was enhanced.
To kiss and fondle her I left the shore.
The water's chill kept me from doing more.

### 4.23

The finest epigrammatist you seek
Of all the best who write their lines in Greek?
Callimachus does yield the highest place
To Bruttianus' wit and verbal grace.
If he in Latin epigram should riddle,
I would in my own tongue play second fiddle.

## 4.27

### TO THE EMPEROR

The praise you have conferred on me
Is ruler's generosity.
My rival takes it as a blow
To his dull lines, so crude and low.
So grant to me a higher prize
And laugh to see his hackles rise.

## 4.28

Fabrics you give your boy of highest sheen,
The richest garments men have ever seen.
You've laden him with all that he can bear.
He'll leave you nude, without a rag to wear.

## 4.29

My poems crowd on one another's heel.
The thronging of them all is what you feel.
They lack acclaim that comes from being rare,
Like lonely rose that braves the winter air.
The dainty mistress can compel our eye,
While over-trafficked drudges make us fly.
So Persius with his precious verses few
Does more than Marsus can with epics do.
So just pretend this book is all I wrote
And grant it merit of a higher note.

#### 4.32

The bee, in amber shut, shines out.
It is a higher fate, no doubt,
In iridescent garb to be
Preserved for all eternity.

#### 4.33

Books deeply studied cram your shelf,
Yet you write nothing of yourself.
You say you must let death sift merit,
Your works are what heirs will inherit.
To earn your fame without delay
Be posthumously praised—today.

#### 4.34

A cloak of dubious glory honors you,
Since, hole by hole, a glorious light shines through.

#### 4.35

Two hornless deer did proudly strut,
Banged head to head with fearsome butt
That dogs fell back from their attack
And hunters' arms their prey did lack.
What made the does, with anger full,
Do battle proper to a bull?

### 4.38

"No" is enticing; so is wooing slow.
But nothing works till you stop saying "No."

### 4.41

You wrap your throat before you launch your song.
Wrapping our ears were best, to muffle wrong.

### 4.42

Let me describe my perfect boy:
Egyptian birth–knows how to toy.
And white–a pricey rarity.
Stars in his eyes–hair floating free,
No curls but combed lasciviously.
A dainty nose, one turned up neat.
His rosy lips for kissing sweet.
He pesters when I don't desire,
Refuses when I am on fire.
Experimentaler than I,
But never giving girls the eye.
Still boy when others think him man,
And doing what for me he can.
You see what makes my judgment sound–
He is the very boy I've found.

4·43

I never said you were a fag.
Absolve me of that uncouth tag.
If I said that, let me drink poison
Or herbs of most imperiled foison.
I swear I did not, come what may.
Let lightning strike without delay.
This is, of all my gibes, the brunt:
I only said that you lick cunt.

4·44

Vesuvius, once latticed with vine shade,
With grapes from which the richest wine was made–
This is where Bacchus had his favorite haunt
And Satyrs could their wildest dances vaunt.
Here Venus more than Sparta made her place,
Here Hercules brought blessings for the race.
What once in beauty and renown was cherished
In fire and ashes has with horror perished.
Were it allowed immortal gods to rue it,
They would have wished they were not doomed to do it.

4·47

This painting burnt him in encaustic stuff.
Was Phaëthon's first firing not enough?

4.48

You do get buggered up your ass,
But weep to see the moment pass.
Because you did not want to do it,
Or that you wish you were not through it?

4.49

You think my epigrams are silly?
Far worse is bombast uttered shrilly–
Like Tereus baking human pie,
Or Daedal son who tried to fly,
Monster-Cyclopes keeping sheep.
My verse is of such nonsense free,
It poses not as tragedy.
But praise for those things does exceed?
Those things men praise–but mine they read.

4.58

Mourning alone, you hide your fears–
The world would see you *have* no tears.

4.59

A snake crawled by a poplar tree
That dropped its amber copiously.
The snake with this congealing stuff
Was covered in a splendor tough,
Which made the place where it was pent
Pass Cleopatra's monument.
For regal pride there is no room–
Your snake lies in a better tomb.

4.70

His father took his lingering last quittance
And left his son the meagerest remittance.
To say he mourned to see his father die,
Before the will was read, would be a lie.

4.76

I did not ask wealth for my own,
But just to make my rival groan.

4.84

Men flock to Thais
    From north and south,
Yet she's a virgin–
    All but her mouth.

4.87

Cold Bassa leans and coos
 At baby's little shoes.
Shows warmth of heart?
 No, masks a fart.

4.89

Slow down, my book, don't race beyond the goal
Or keep on trotting like a frisky foal.
You've used up all the paper in this roll.
Continuing, you'd make me lose control.
The reader says you might have gone too far,
My scribe says, "Hold your horses where they are."

# BOOK FIVE

### 5.2

Ladies, lads, and virgins pure,
I offer you my book demure.
Those looking for my dirty lines
Must scrounge for things from other times.
This book is for the Emperor, gratis,
To read in presence of his goddess.


### 5.4

She drinks, but would conceal it,
    Breath mints will leave no hint?
But veins inflamed reveal it.
    "She's drunk again—on mint."

## 5.5
### TO THE EMPEROR'S LIBRARIAN

Preserver of Domitian's books,
Sorting his volumes into nooks
Please put me in some minor place
Where comic poets play with grace.
But for the writings of Himself–
Virgil alone can share that shelf.

## 5.6
### TO THE EMPEROR'S CHAMBERLAIN

I would not trouble you, who guard the Presence,
But take the chance of praying, at your pleasance,
I could all nuisances of yours at once dispel,
And join your worthy son to wish you well;

You know your master's high serenity
When he would show innate benignity,
On those who would extend a culture's fame
Without persistence justly drawing blame.

Please find a time to offer my work, shyly
And not as anything you value highly.
Extend it with a shrug, not hoping much,
As if you had whole groaning shelves of such.

I've made my book as pretty as can be,
Befitting what an Emperor might see.
And given his high standing with the Muses,
He might contrive to find for it some uses.

### 5·7
#### ROME REBORN FROM FIRE

The Phoenix is reborn from fire
To live a thousand years or higher.
Thus Rome, its former beauty burned,
Is to its earlier form returned–
So, Vulcan, threats of fires reduce
Against Mars, though he did seduce
Your Venus. Though you chained them then,
Restore their amity again.
Remember how Mars fights for Rome,
But Venus claims it for her own.

### 5·9

The doctor arrived, precipitous,
With interns all solicitous.
Their hands were like the North Wind, so
That now I burn with fever's glow.

### 5.10

Why do people hold their praise
To heap it on "the good old days"?
To dead men they are far more giving,
But envy undermines the living.
New temples cannot match the old,
Whose glory is in legends told.
So Virgil was no Ennius.
They treated even Homer thus.
Menander was called second-rate,
And Ovid only pleased his mate.
If I must die to get my fame,
I gladly will put off the same.

### 5.11

#### TO A POET-JEWELER

His fingers deftly shape rare stone,
Yet turn out verses of his own.
The gems he wears are true delights,
But nothing to the gems he writes.

### 5.13

Though I am poor, I was born free,
And those well-known in Rome know me.
They see me passing in the street
And like a famous person greet.
You have a multicolumned home,
And many debtors throughout Rome.
A freedman with vast hordes in fee,
And foreign lands too vast to see.
Thus high, you never will go higher.
Nor to my heights can you aspire.

### 5.15

This is the fifth book of my verse,
And no one has by them fared worse.
Some have, in fact, won greater fame,
By being coupled to my name.
This brings me little or no pay,
But joy at saying what I may.

5.16

As lawyer I could draw a fee,
Instead of writing distichs free.
You keep me at my versifying
By praises there is no denying,
Still, once assumed, a legal case
My debt would instantly erase.
And now my poems roam the town,
And earn me nothing but renown.
At least when Virgil gave men joy,
They gave him his desired love-boy.
You draw your purse strings even tighter?
I'll turn a reader, not a writer.


5.17

You boast a bloodline so refined,
No commoner can wed your kind.
My lowliness earns no regard–
But did I wed a bodyguard?


5.18

It's gift time–do not think that I will send
The holiday's best presents without end.
I send a little offspring of my brain,
Which can do nothing more than entertain.
Rich gifts are like a fisher's baited line
To land a bigger fish in later time.
To ask such from a writer would be hateful.
For what the poet *does* you should be grateful.

5.29

You give me carrots as a gift—
　They will expand my brain.
Why did you not keep them,
　So you could have that gain?


5.32

Dying he went the earth beneath
And did his debts, not wealth, bequeath.


5.33

A lawyer calls my versifying thin?
Just wait till that verse "cross-examines" him!


5.34

My parents in the underworld! I send
This servant girl—take care and gently tend.
Conduct her past the terrifying shade.
Keep her of circling horrors unafraid,
For she, alas, was only six days shy
Of six years when too soon she came to die.
Protect her as she plays her childhood games,
And lisps, as she was wont, our names.
Earth, sadly mounded on this gravesite new,
Press lightly on her, as she did on you.

## 5.36

Some published praise I wrought
   To do his bidding.
He says he owes me nought,
   But who's he kidding?

## 5.37

Her voice was poignant as a swan's last song,
Her skin soft as wool tendrils stroked out long.
Delicious as sweet oysters from the lake,
More precious than the gems that jewelers make,
Whiter than ivory, fresher than the snow,
And pure as where the finest lilies blow,
Her hair more filigreed than floating flower,
Her mouth wafts odors like a fragrant bower,
She can in beauty prove the peacock's tutor,
Than Phoenix rarer, or than squirrel cuter–
Such was my darling, not quite six in years,
Who now must under earth cope with her fears–
My little solace, stimulant, and joy,
Who never reached an age to meet a boy.
Yet Paetus claims I mourn not manfully,
When I can see in him true tragedy.
He lost a wife, and has to live without her
Who bore such grace (and wealthy goods) about her.
He bravely forges on without his wife–
Who left him umpteen millions for life!

### 5.42

A thief can rifle any till,
A fire with ash your home can fill,
A creditor calls in your debt.
Bad harvest does your farm upset,
An impish mistress robs your dwelling,
Storm shatters ships with water swelling.
But gifts to friends your friendships save.
You keep thus always what you gave.

### 5.43

Her teeth look whiter than they ought.
Of course they should—the teeth were bought.

### 5.45

You say that you are beautiful and young.
A song that's always by the old crones sung.

### 5.46

My amorous demands require
I whip you to provoke desire.
Yet you, my boy, I sadly see
Fear not the lashes, nor love me.

### 5.47

There's crazy truth in what I heard him say:
    "I never dine alone"—gregarious feat!
He only eats when other people pay.
    When he's alone, at home, he does not eat.

### 5.50

You make it an affront
   When I'm not feeding you.
My kitchen cannot glow
   Without your heating too.
Stop sniffing at my door
   To see if there's been cooking.
You treat that as a theft
   Beyond your overlooking.
You think it is a crime
   Whenever you're not eating.
But even outlaws bold
   Are cut some slack for cheating.

### 5.51

He's always laden down
With every book in town.
To write all he does know
He keeps scribes in his tow.
As wise man he would pose,
Know all that Cato knows.
But bid him say hello,
No answer will he show.
He will not deign to speak
In Latin or in Greek.

### 5.52

You are my patron, I would give you praise.
But when talk of your virtues I would raise,
I'm told you have already laid them out.
Where I would whisper, you your merits shout.
We must more prudently divide our labor
To have efficient impact on our neighbor.
If I'm to praise you, you must hold your peace,
Or give me from my gratitude release.
Your gifts do not give me the power to do
Promotion constantly undone by you.
You undermine my prized veracity
With puffings of your own loquacity.

### 5.53

Your lines are labored, far too superficial–
The learned myths they treat are artificial.
Give up Medeas, sacrilegious dinners,
And all the tales of innovative sinners.
To make your poetry appropriate,
Some *natural* catastrophes relate.

### 5.54

My orator is tongue-tied–at a meeting
Wrote not the name he should be greeting.

### 5.57

I call you "Boss"? Don't show wild joy.
That's what I call my slaves' head boy.

### 5.58

You think tomorrow will be your reward.
It's what you shape your fond hopes toward.
But where has it been hiding as days thronged?
If it comes next, why was today prolonged?
Tomorrow, not yet born, is old as Nestor.
Or Priam, who had fifty sons to pester.
We pay for joys—what do you pay for it?
Its bidding date is past, too late to fit.
Forget tomorrow's teasing long delay.
To make life pleasant, dwell on yesterday.

### 5.59

Thank me you get no wealthy gifts from me.
It keeps you of reciprocation free.

### 5.60

You try to prod me into verse,
Your private doings to rehearse.
You would have fame at any price—
The showing, even, of your vice.
But you deserve no verse's naming,
Not even in by deft defaming.
In no way will this scoundrel live
The afterlife my lashings give.
Let poets of his own degree,
Who lack my own gentility,
Accommodate that fawning bitch.
I will not scratch his scabrous itch.

### 5.66

You never offer me to greet.
Remind me we must never meet.

### 5.71

**TO MARK ANTONY**

The worst death you contrived
   Was Cicero's harsh end.
The man of treasured words
   To silence you did send.

Your purchased agent with his sword
   That honorable head assailed,
Triumphing over eloquence
   Where even Catiline had failed.

This is the just reward
   For your transgression grim:
Since you tore out his tongue,
   All tongues will speak of him.

### 5.74

Each son of Pompey has a separate tomb,
Nor can be said to warrant ampler room.
But Pompey cannot be so closely pent.
He's covered, aptly, by a continent.

### 5.76

A king to arsenic became immune
With graduated dosings, spoon by spoon.
He put them in the dishes he was carving–
So stingy meals keep you, by steps, from starving.

### 5.77

Great men voraciously you heed–
With them no hearing aid you need.

### 5.79

He says he sweats so as he dines
That he must to his wardrobe go.
It gives him opportunity betimes
The range of all his clothes to show.

Yet I sit sweatless through the meal,
And no discomfort do I feel.
Why am I cool in every air?
I have a single suit to wear.

### 5.81

Vainly the poor extend their palms.
Only the rich are given alms.

5.83

I fly when you pursue me,
But when you shy, I woo thee.
Explain it to me, can't you,
Why I must ever want to want you.

# BOOK SIX

### 6.1

I offer this (sixth) volume to myself
For polishing before it leaves the shelf.
If I can shape it up and make it fit,
It may not faint if Caesar looks on it.


### 6.5

I need more millions for the house I want,
And ask a loan you tell me you won't grant.
My credit's bad, you say—well, naturally,
Were I in cash, would I be begging thee?


### 6.6

Your lady's with the art scene all aglow.
To theater she is devoted so,
That, after screwing each star in the show,
To players of the "smallest parts" she'll go.

6.7

Caesar would make our women marry men,
But ten is overdoing it, by ten.
To marry wholesale does not make a bride,
But pushes the hardworking whores aside.


6.8

When she was wooed by Marquis This and That,
Her guardian gave to both these toffs their hat,
In favor of a waste-disposal heir.
He knew who had the greatest change to spare.


6.12

The coif she wears she claims she grew.
Does that seem splitting hairs to you?


6.13

Suzanne is like a sculptor's masterpiece,
A thing to rival all the arts of Greece.
Like marble shines the brilliance in her face,
Her bearing softly brings out every grace.
The magic belt of Venus she coaxed free
From Cupid, who was hoarding it with glee.
Should Venus need it to seduce her Jove,
She'll have to filch it back from Suzanne's trove.

### 6.14

You claim you are a poet true
　　But don't have time to write.
Is that what genuine poets do?
　　Yeah, right!

### 6.15

A drop of amber hit an ant,
　　While crawling past a tree.
A brief and trifling thing preserved
　　For all eternity.

### 6.16

Priapus frightens thieves and fags
　　With his enormous penis.
So ward all plunderers away,
　　And welcome friends of Venus.

### 6.18

They buried him in Spain.
　　'Twas where he met his fate.
But you he left behind,
　　His fame to celebrate.

### 6.19

We are in court for no high politics–
A thief ensnared our goats with his sly tricks.
Since, lawyer, you despise a case so low,
You trumpet famous names for pompous show.
Leave off your Cato, drop your Manlius,
Give notice to our simple goats–and us.

### 6.20

You asked, "What can I do for you?"
I said a simple loan would do.
You stalled, excused, and hesitated,
With artistry procrastinated.
Your "Yes" was blocked and tortured so,
I said, "For God's sake, tell me no."

### 6.21

As Venus made of two a wedded one,
She told the bride: "My gift you may not shun."
But to the groom she promised deepest woe,
Should he in time unfaithful conduct show:
"My Mars, before he wed me, fooled around,
For which his head I would condignly pound.
But when I made him husband true,
A better mate he was than Juno knew."
Him, with her little whip, she deftly tamed.
(I'd rather be by her forever lamed.)

6.22

You marry, late, your paramour?
You cannot so your crime abjure.

6.23

You want my cock at full attention
If sex you casually mention?
No matter how you coax men's tools,
Hand "makes a motion" face o'errules.

6.26

His head cannot its new task shirk,
His tongue's employed where prick won't work.

6.31

Your doctor is now treating your wife's–cough?
You might as well plead, "Doctor, take me off."

6.33

Poor Matho is a walking accident,
His home, his goods, his pansies from him rent.
He has no more a pretty boy he sucks.
He's reached the last extremity–he fucks.

6.34

Kiss hard and often as you might.
How many kisses call I right?
How can I count the waves that roll,
Or bees that make a stunning toll,
Or shouts or huzzahs in the throng
That usher Caesar's way along,
Or kisses astronomical
Catullus rallied to his call?
Don't ask of me exact amount.
Some things go far beyond a count.

6.36

A bent huge nose, a monstrous cock to match,
Curved each into the other, what a snatch!

6.40

No woman was more beautiful than you.
   No woman is more beautiful than she.
I wanted once the joy we knew.
   In her, want what you used to be.

6.48

Don't let the cheers go to your head—
They're only for the feast you spread.

6.52

He was to shears and razors native born.
His customers were magically shorn.
He shaved men who could never feel his hand,
And made unruly locks in order stand.
Rest easy, earth, upon one loved so much.
You cannot lighter lie than was his touch.

6.57

On your bald pate no wig you use.
You draw hairs on, with no excuse.
At least no barber needs to trim it.
You can erase it in a minute.

6.60

He reads my verses, just to be in fashion,
But finds himself whipsawed by sudden passion.
He frowns, then chortles–chokes at what he reads–
And calls them the most infamous of screeds,
Then he goes pale, as under some indicting–
You've got him, poems! That's what I call writing.

6.63

With subterfuge he's scheming for your money,
Abundantly you see him spreading honey.
Yet in your will you still are listing him
As if he bound you to his every whim.
You say, "He sends expensive presents here"–
As though fish had no hidden hook to fear!
You think that he will weeping see you die?
Just cut off his allowance, and he'll cry.

6.66

The auction master could not close
For slave girl of a sluttish pose.
To show her unobtrusive charms,
He took her fondly in his arms
And lusty kisses did renew–
The lowest bidder then withdrew.

6.71

His slave girl could a saintly patriarch stun,
Seduce an old man burying his son.
But now his former temptress blights his life:
He sold her as his slave–bought as his wife.

### 6.82

A stranger eyed me narrowly,
As if to buy (or tailor) me.
"Could you that poet, Martial, be,
Whom aesthetes praise so learnedly?
But if so, why so poorly dressed?"
"Poets are poor, and often stressed."
So, patron, since you are not broke,
Save this poor poet–send a cloak!

### 6.90

She has a single lover true,
But counts (alas) of husbands two.

### 6.91

The law proclaims now, "Take one wife, not many."
Then happy you, who never wanted any.

### 6.98

Thais smells worse than caustic oil,
Or corpses rotting in the soil,
Or rotten eggs, or rutting goats,
Or swill that's vomited by stoats.
To hide the odor, Thais drenches
Her body with distracting stenches.
But worse than ointments on her shelf,
The smell most dreadful is–herself.

# BOOK SEVEN

7.3

You ask me why I send you not my book?
For fear you'll say, "Here's my work–take a look."


7.4

Haggard? To vice does owe it?
No–claims that he's a poet.


7.9

This lawyer has the learning and the years,
But never learned to tickle jurors' ears.


7.11

You want a few corrections in my hand
To fit my book for peddling at the stand.

### 7.14

Fate humbles her, she's lost her pet,
　　No bird by soft Catullus sung,
No dove plunged to a hell of jet,
　　Whose praises stretch the poet's lung.
Rather, a mite of few years yet,
　　But mightily already hung.


### 7.16

My house is out of funds—all things I lack
Except your presents. Want to buy them back?


### 7.18

Your face entices, and your thighs—
Why are you shunned by all the guys?
Because when in your cunt they drill,
Its liquids clack and gurgle, shrill.
You hold your tongue—no other part
Will sound off (not a single fart).
But cunt keeps up its squish and squeal
Of gibberish without repeal.
You hope your men will cease to balk?
Then teach that lower mouth to talk.

7.25

Your epigrams are really nice,
With nothing in them to entice.
They burble on as smooth as syrup,
And nothing there to prick the ear up.
They're whiter than a mimic's mask.
So why do you for hearers ask?
Where you should be a vice-decrier,
You give a baby's pacifier.
For me, no lullabies I sing.
I want harsh lines that have a sting.

7.30

Barbarian hordes en masse you fuck,
Odd types into your bed you tuck,
You take on blacks and Asian forces,
And Jews, and soldiers, and their horses.
Yet you, voracious Roman chick,
Have never known a Roman dick.

7.38

This slave's a monster with a hairy face,
The other takes up just as much grim space.
So put the two together in one breath,
And each will scare the other half to death.

## 7.41

You pose as cosmopolitan. Prophetic?
Not really metaphysical. Cosmetic.

## 7.46

You send your presents with your home-made verse,
Which wearies you, afflicts me even worse.
Give poems with your presents to the wealthy.
Send prose to me if you would keep me healthy.

## 7.51

You like my verse, but would not buy?
Then give my lawyer friend a try.
He does not quote, he *is*, my book.
To find a thing, you need not look,
You'll find it easily in him,
Who treats each poem as a hymn.
He could in fact my fame purloin
By passing it as his own coin.
But he proclaims it is *my* verse
He does so endlessly rehearse.
So wait till his law work is done–
He'll not a dinner with you shun.
He'll sing my lines relentlessly–
You'll end up asking to be free
Of poetry, and surcease ask,
But still your patience he will task.

7·54

Your dreams of me give direful omens
My troubles will be less than no men's.
I bribe the soothsayer with wine
To tell me what rites to make mine.
She tells me what to sacrifice,
And doubts my money will suffice.
Before she takes off all I own,
Sleep not! Or keep your dreams unknown.

7·58

To give that man my book were risky.
He must like learned tomes, less frisky.
But if perchance he does already know it,
To Washington himself I'd show it.

7·59

You've six or seven husbands had,
But each yearned for a lusty lad.
Their cocks stand not for any women,
No matter how you pump or prim 'em.
You dumped each one, but only found
No others for your purpose sound.
Why not in low dives look about
To find some hairy burly lout?
But even there a doubt still nags—
Some burly louts have proven fags.

7.62

You screw the handsome boys and ask
That others witness to the task.
By letting others see you *act*
You hide what's *done* to you in fact.

7.65

From court to court you annually trudge,
And never get a favorable judge.
Instead of spending years in case reviews,
Why not just take the wiser course–and lose?

7.75

With her looks, "giving out" will never do.
It takes her *monetary* giving too.

7.81

"Your book has thirty epigrams unneeded."
I've only thirty clunkers? I've succeeded.

7.83

Just as the barber moved to shave cheek two,
The first cheek's whiskers bristled up anew.

7.85

You wrote some clever couplets? "Take a look."
These epigrams are fine–but not a book.

7.90

Dour Matho offers me a "mixed review,"
To which contentedly I answer, "Whew!"
Most poets get reviews that are unmixed,
With every verse and stanza in them nixed.

# BOOK EIGHT

8.1

My book, you'll join the company
Of conquering divinity.
Be moral now, and forswear lust.
Speak not a thing that is not just.

8.3

Why write five books, or more, write six,
And keep my Muse performing tricks?
Whose fame by now is more than mine?
Of my work all can quote a line.
At life's end many men will go
Reciting me in realms below.
Are there more fields for me to know?
Give schoolmasters some heavy stuff
To make his students' lives more rough?
Or tune my lines to martial measure
To blast away the arts of leisure?
Let others do such boring work,
Whom my light wit would merely irk.
I deal with life, and make it see
What comes of all its flummery.
My instrument with tunes will glow
That blaring trumpets dare not blow.

8.5

All medals bright bestowed on you for merit,
Your mistresses for love gifts will inherit.

8.6

He gives his goblets an encomium,
Says nothing's tastier than the foam in 'em,
But when at last he calls us in to sup,
He serves us raw wine in a wooden cup.

8.7

Why ask for greater time to make your case,
Who never move at more than sluggish pace?
You endlessly spin out your thoughts too few.
No one can say more and be silent too.

8.10

The richest clothes he takes away
At bargain rates, his critics say.
What makes them cheap? He will not pay.

8.12

A wealthy wife is not for me,
For she'd enforce docility.
A wife must her man's will enact,
Or else there is no wedding pact.

8.13

I bought a slave to be my fool.
I'm gypped. He's putting me to school.

8.14

Your trees you keep in greenhouse warm,
Your guest room is exposed to storm.
The outside comes so quick inside,
The North Wind could not here abide.
Now listen to my shivering pleas:
Treat me as kindly as your trees.

### 8.17

I was your lawyer, and I made your plea,
But now you fob me off with half my fee.
"You lost the case!" intemperately you swore.
To serve you I lost honor, which is more.

### 8.18

Your poems, if you published them, would shine
And seem to all far wittier than mine.
But out of friendship you promote my glory,
Though yours could make an honorable story.
Thus Virgil would not lyrics write like Horace,
Or vie with Varius in tragic chorus.
Some friends will give up goods or yield their gold.
But few will let their own worth go untold.

### 8.19

He claims rich status, but with straitened means.
The last point is more honest than it seems.

### 8.20

He turns out verses by the ton,
But never publishes a one.
He is too dumb to be a poet,
But wise enough in fact to know it.

### 8.22

You say you're serving boar, but give me pig.
You really think the difference is not big?

### 8.23

For cooking ill I beat my slave.
You say that brands me as a knave.
You draw me to a greater treason–
To beat my slave *without* a reason.

### 8.25

When I was sick you made one visit only.
I hope in time to make you far less lonely.

### 8.27

With wheedling gifts, with hoverings-by,
Your heirs all say, in dumb show, "Die!"

### 8.29

My works charm, taken verse by stinging verse.
Can they, collected in a book, seem worse?

### 8.35

How can your squabbling be so curst?
Of natural pairings yours is first–
Worst husband with a wife that's worst.

### 8.43

They each took separate spouses to their bed,
Then swiftly to the graveyard each they led.
Conjoining both their marriage feats,
They'll serve each other funeral meats.

8.44

Live now! A minute later is too late.
No child should in his schoolroom wait.
Yet you are old and haven't started living.
You trudge to patrons, hoping they'll be giving.
In all the marts you fill the business hours
With sniffing everywhere for random dowers.
You crawl, ingratiate, and basely plead,
With hope at last to satiate your greed.
No matter how much secret coin you store,
Or loans accumulate in hope for more,
Your heirs will say you left a small estate,
With little comfort as they weigh their fate.
Consider this: As soon as your will's read,
Some heir will take your lover-boy to bed.

8.46

You, like Hippolytus, a virgin boy,
Are shy, your blushing beauty cannot cloy.
The chaste Diana would to you succumb,
And Cybel would to you in longing come.
Yet you, in spite, give men nothing but misses
Whenever they can tease from you some kisses.
Well, blessed be the wife that wins you over
And fools her husband with so sweet a lover.

8.47

Bristly here, and smooth that place–
Who would suppose a single face?

8.54

You're beautiful and sinful—in a trice
I'd settle for less looks to get less vice.


8.60

The Statue you could be of Liberty
Could you but lose a foot, or two, or three.


8.63

He takes my poet friend's delightful boy.
And now he takes away *my* blooming joy.
No poet, he is certain, does he slight,
But honors as he takes each catamite.


8.64

For birthday givings you your life relate
To get gifts on a fixed rotating date.
Accumulating births confute your youth,
Their tabulation is of little truth.
Your birthdays mount up high as Nestor's muster—
Then how can you retain your boyhood luster?
If you keep birthdays winter, spring, and fall,
We must conclude you were not born at all.


8.69

You honor poets of an ancient name,
And give only the dead a living fame.
And so, consistently, as is your wont,
You'd honor me if I would die—I won't.

8.74

Eye doctoring was your first claim,
Then boxing gave you greater fame.
You have in fact one enterprise–
In both roles, you were poking eyes.

8.79

With women you keep company
Who are as ugly as can be.
These ancient frights you take along
To show off in your social throng.
You hope that we will make compare,
So even *you* look young and fair.

8.81

She swears not by the gods but by her jewels.
A love for them her total thinking fuels.
Should they be taken from her inner being,
There is no point in further objects seeing.
To live without them she no longer can–
Where is our needed second-story man?

# BOOK NINE

## Introduction

My little verses you may trifles call,
But this is poetry that fills the hall.
Let others more majestic structures raise–
My nothings are what wins me instant praise.


### 9.4

She charges little for a fuck.
For little more, she'll deftly suck.
Since for so little you can screw her,
What makes you be so lavish to her?
"While others fuck, and suck, and gab,
Her artistry is not to blab."


### 9.9

You like to eat abroad, but act the lout.
With loutish ways, you won't dine out.

### 9.10

She's wise to marry such a guy.
He's wiser still—he won't comply.

### 9.15

For seven husbands dead, all tombstones read:
THIS GRAVE DID CHLOE MAKE. She did indeed.

### 9.21

His boy he traded for a farm—it seems
Each man in this transaction gained his dreams:
Where one of them now reaps, the other reams.

### 9.25

We eye your handsome slave boy, Hyllus,
As sun and stars with awe do fill us.
All men are moved by searing beauty,
Why make reproaching this your duty?
If you ban ogling his behind,
Invite no guests except the blind.

### 9.32

My girl can be an easy lay,
If one I never have to pay.
I'll keep her though she's done my slave,
Or if she does a threesome crave.
But if she blabs, or asks for coin,
Let her a cock less choosy join.

9.33

The critics in the Baths rain bravos thick
For Marcus' coup de théâtre–his dick.


9.35

You peddle gossip, false or true,
And which is which, none knows but you.
You chronicle the wars not fought,
And what dim diplomats have sought.
You tell us who is screwing whom,
And hope to entertain the room.
Such "news" will invitations bring?
We'll feed you, but don't say a thing.


9.37

You are assembled from the marketplace.
You shop for the ingredients of your face.
Your hair is shaped in distant styling schools,
Your teeth are stored in various reticules.
At night your separate parts lie under latch.
The eyebrows, that you ogle with, detach.
Your cunt, so overworked, has predeceased you.
Your every seeming charm has long been leased you.
I'd never lie with you–or, far less, do it.
My cock's one squinting eye has seen clear through it.

9.41

Your left hand is your mistress at your call,
But it provides you no male heirs at all.
One coupling gave Horatius children three,
And Mars bred heirs to flock around his knee.
Had they just coupled with their sterile hands
We would have lacked our patriotic bands.
For martial reasons reconsider then:
You left hand squirts out nonexistent men.

9.46

His buildings gobble up such sums,
The scaffolding exceeds his funds.
And yet he is still in his senses,
Ask him to loan–he'll plead, "Expenses!"

9.47

You can philosophers recite,
And wear their beard, and rant all night.
But what philosophers in kind
Lodge any cocks in their behind?
Say what profound curriculum
Makes scholars keep a dick in 'em?

9.50

You call my poems doggerel,
So simple, yet they cast a spell.
Your works are crammed with martial noise,
While I make up enticing boys.
Your giants all are made of clay,
While mine breathe deep of everyday.


9.52

My birthday I hold dear,
But yours I hold more near.
Mine gave me living,
Yours is more giving.


9.53

Your birthday I would hail with something pleasant,
But you demur, and say, "I want no present."
You leave me of all obligation free.
You ask me not to give to you? Give me!


9.56

This boy goes out on campaign bearing arms
To keep his master ready to fend harms.
And he no weapon carries as his own
But his soft-wounding spear not fully grown.
It is enough to make a girl or boy
Writhe, sorrowing from put-off joy.
So let him not campaign in foreign lands.
He should a warrior prove in native hands.

### 9.57

His cloak is worn–how can it hold together?
Worn as a bronze vase beaten by the weather,
Worn as a convict's shins the shackles chafe,
Worn as a mule's neck yoked to make it safe.
In contrast with this cloak (there is no hassle),
The only thing more deep-worn is his asshole.

### 9.62

She wears a fetid robe, as if to say,
It is the robe, not she, that smells that way.

### 9.63

For dinners you ask all the fags to knock.
But is that dining when you feed just cock?

### 9.66

Reward for having children you demand.
Why not just *have* them–if you can?

### 9.67

I had a frisky girl complying,
And boylike on her stomach lying.
And next made of her mouth my drudge–
And all of this I firmly judge
Of turpitude entirely free,
Since I refused when she asked me
On equal terms to service her–
A service *you* would not defer.

9.69
You, poked in front, extrude behind.
If poked in back, what would we find?


9.76
This painting of a boy the father cherished
Was finished twenty years before he perished.
He died just when he first had shaved his beard,
The moment when the Fates his life-thread sheared.
No other image did his father save
Than ashes brought back from his exploits brave.
The painting will his memory renew,
But here I paint him, in my words, more true.


9.77
He writes a pansy poem
   On the perfect dinner party.
To make a dinner perfect,
   Cut out the arty-farty.


9.78
Dead husbands she can seven reckon.
Now she weds *him*. The seven beckon.


9.81
My books are praised by him who reads,
Though critics damn them in their screeds.
But who's to judge a proper meat—
Another cook, or those who eat?

## 9.83

We see the wonders and we thank you more
  For games now mounted in the Colosseum.
For those who ranted publicly before
  Are forced to shut up if they want to see 'em.

## 9.89

You ask verse from us after serving food.
And then relent: "You need not make it good."

## 9.97

Black envy eats his soul—my book succeeds.
My praises tear him daily when he reads.
I'm made a knight—and envy eats his soul.
My house is lavish—envy eats his soul.
My fame grows more—he envies what men say.
His envy will at last eat him away.

## 9.98

The rain that soaks the vineyards through
Will fill his casks with water too.

# BOOK TEN

**10.1**

If this book seems too long,
Just read from it one song.
In this way, whittling it
And reading bit by bit,
A little book with ease
You make it, as you please.

10.4

You long for classic arms and war,
Medea deep in children's gore,
Icarian plungings in the sea,
And any dire monstrosity.
Why seek out esoteric rages
When normal life is in my pages?
Unlike your dire demented strife,
My verses have the tang of life.
But you don't want yourself to know
In mirrors that my lines can show.
To dwell on all the guff that was,
Stick to encyclopedias.


10.8

So Paula wants to find a mate?
Antiques are valued by their date.
She's not yet old enough to rate.


10.9

I'm known for firecracker syllables,
For writing lines with witty fillables.
Despite this spreading book publicity,
More know a winning racehorse than know me.

### 10.15

There's no friend who cares more for me, you say.
What presents, then, from you have come my way?
No cash, though it your every pocket fills.
No food, from farmland that your workstaff tills.
No cloak to wear, when winter does me chafe.
No coin extracted from your groaning safe.
What proof have I you've taken up my part–
You feel at ease enough with me to fart?

### 10.16

His arrow, straying, hit his wealthy wife?
He never missed a target in his life.

### 10.18

A bureaucrat enjoys my works,
And his deep cosmic projects shirks?
Forswears voluminous reports,
For my quick wit and dry retorts?
I must your guilt, my Muse, berate–
You block the progress of the state.

### 10.21

You make your audience grope and tarry–
Your reader's not a dictionary.
But commentators I make merry
Who read me with no commentary.

### 10.22

You ask me why I wrap my face.
To shun that person's dread embrace.

### 10.23

He ages with a great serenity,
Who can with what he is contented be.
No act he has performed will haunt him now,
And nothing in the future will him cow.
He never does deplore life's brevity.
For virtue is itself longevity.
Each day recalled does ancient comforts bring.
He lives twice, living and remembering.

### 10.29

The presents you once sent to me she gets,
Your mistress with my plate her table sets.
Tell me, at least, how can you count this just,
My gifts, withheld, finance your costless lust?

### 10.30

You sell such rotten wines to Rome,
No wonder you can't call it home.

### 10.39

You tell your age, but understate it far.
By dating it from star-signs circular.
You had to have been brought to birth that day
Prometheus first made humans out of clay.

10.40

She told me, my misdoubts to end,
She had a nice castrated friend.
But soon I found I was misled–
When I discovered them in bed.

10.41

Your husband why divorce, who's doing fine?
Is it because you're thinking, "But where's mine?"
His buying votes was sucking up the cash,
Leaving your gowns and jewels in a stash.
And when you found out, angry, where the rest went,
You came to see divorce as shrewd investment.

10.42

Your hint of beard just barely is,
It is a froth, a breath, a fizz.
A sunbeam or a wandering breeze
Displaces it with nudging ease.
Girls brush it with a dainty thumb
That sweeps the down off from a plum.
And when you give me kisses free,
Your shadowy beard dusts off on me.

10.43

You planted seven wives under your fields.
No farmer harvests greater (richer) yields.

10.45

If my lines swoon and croon a bit,
You ask for angry acid wit.
You think I have soft flowers sown
Where you prefer to gnaw a bone.
You call for something else, not mine,
For biting vinegar, not wine.

10.46

You want to be all fashion, all things new.
Can you not bear to say a plain thing too?
Say anything, say naught, or say a dumb thing,
But, in a final reckoning, say *some*thing.

10.47

A life so blest you would put none before it?
Some money, just enough you can ignore it.
Some fertile fields on your producing farm
And hearth ablaze within to keep you warm.
No lawsuits, no bought formal wear, no hassle.
A body trim, without a trainer's wrastle.
A mind secure, with trusting friends not silly.
A house with taste designed, not frilly.
Nights drinking deep, but not to stupor given.
A bedmate warm, but not to frenzy driven.
A sleep not enervating that renews.
A sense of what you are in all your views.
A wish to wish no other thing ahead.
Acceptance that in time you must be dead.

### 10.53

I was the noted chariot driver.
No other's fame had been aliver.
In person I was too short-lived.
But all my triumphs have survived.

### 10.55

She can a hard cock accurately weigh
And tell, when soft, what heft has limped away.
Her hand is good enough to work retail.
Hers is, in fact, no hand. It is a scale.

### 10.63

You, reader of this monument,
Regard a life with honor spent.
From five prized sons my fame derives,
And daughters five, who closed my eyes.
I was by gods divinely lucked,
And never but by one man fucked.

### 10.75

I paid her hundreds in my lust,
   To slake it.
She aged toward half that payment, just
   To make it.
Now *she'll* pay freely, if she must—
   (Won't take it.)

### 10.77

That rotter's death came all too swift about.
A fumbling doctor should have dragged it out.

### 10.81

Both lovers raced and in upon her burst–
Each with the hope that he would have her first.
She thought she could to both demands be kind.
One fucked her front, one pronged her from behind.

### 10.83

Your hairs are carefully disposed
Lest your bald pate should be disclosed.
But winds lift them in wavy drifts,
Moved in a blur of constant shifts.
How can you have so little hair,
Yet have it show up everywhere?

### 10.84

Why will he never go to bed?
Just see by whom he would be led.

### 10.90

Stop fingering your cunt. Time to forget it.
That's stirring ashes never to be wetted.
Young girls may do't, or older types still wombed.
But you're no longer simply old, you're tombed.

10.95

Your lover and your spouse agree on this:
That baby that you got cannot be his.

10.97

He made his preparations sound,
With relatives all gathered round.
His burial clothes were now laid out,
Of his last will there was no doubt–
To me his whole estate he'd give.
But then the cheat resolved–to live.

10.102

A man who never has with women lain,
    How can he plausibly be called a father?
Yet you aspire to have a poet's name
    And think to write a single line's a bother.

# BOOK ELEVEN

**II.2**

Haughty morals, take a powder!
Naughty verse, sing ever louder!
Cato go, Poor Richard's dicta,
Propriety and all things stricter.
This is a book for carnival,
Which Nerva will not mind at all.
You people of the wild stuff wary,
Sit down and read the dictionary.
Such sobersides are not for me.
I'll keep my book of morals free.

11.3

I write not only for sophisticates,
For intellectuals with learned mates.
On frontiers wild, and even in far Britain,
Troops quote my epigrams with lips frost-bitten.
But this regard fills not my money pouch
However I keep proving I'm no slouch.
They say this is a new Augustan age,
But no Maecenases support my page.


11.8

Aroma ling'ring in a jar,
Or pine scent wafted from afar,
Or apples kept for winter eating,
Or spring trees fresh for lovers' meeting,
Or closet rustling with silk gowns,
Or amber warmed in virgin's mounds,
A red wine of the finest vintage,
Or blooms with bees astride the windage,
Perfume shops, altars' incensed air,
Or petals from ambrosial hair,
Why list such odors? All combine,
In that boy's kisses I call mine.
You casually ask his name–
You think that I am that insane?

## 11.9

### PORTRAIT OF THE DRAMATIST

A front like Jove's—the theater at Rome:
This painting gives to both a home.

## 11.10

### GENEROUS COLLEAGUE

In satire he excels, why not in plays?
Because he would not crimp his brother's praise.

## 11.13

Whoever passes on this well-worn way
Before the noble monument make stay.
For this was Paris, in his art sublime—
The greatest mime of his or any time—
And buried with him in this earth
Are earthy talent, tears, and mirth.
He smote the heart of Venus and her lad.
Look on, and with the world be sad.

## 11.15

I wrote some things that catered to the prudes.
But now I'll deck my pages out with nudes.
To make my past endeavors all look prim,
To wine and drunkenness I'll raise a hymn.
My lines I'll drench in unguents and devices
For luring girls and laddies to all vices.
I'll name outright, and not pretend a shock,
What even pious Numa called his cock–
What none of us can prudishly disclaim,
Because it is the spring from which we came.
But I will comic license still invoke,
To serve me as my reputation's cloak.

## 11.16

Persnickety readers, time to leave!
I now write stuff to make you grieve.
My toga off, my lines will jiggle
And with the belly-dancer wriggle.
Now what we wear will ask no pardon
For standing out with sculptured hard-on.
To make the Founding Fathers horny,
And Boston matrons less than thorny–
They'll lather up between their thighs
And wonder at their fellows' size.
Of course Lucretia will not look
Till Brutus goes–then: Seize the book!

11.17

Let not my midnight verses you dismay.
You'll find a few that you can read by day.


11.19

She has grammatical pretensions?
My cock can't run through all declensions.


11.20

Caesar himself can dirty verses proffer.
He told how Fulvia made him an offer
To get revenge upon Mark Antony,
She told sublime Augustus to feel free
To fuck her as her husband's penalty.
He said that this for vengeance would not pass.
Would he comply if asked to fuck man's ass?
She threatened, if unfucked, to raise war's strife.
He said his cock he would defend, like life.
You see what warrant this gives to my lines:
Who calls my verse less chaste than the Divine's?

## 11.21

Her cunt–broad as an asshole that you
Might spot on some equestrian statue–
Is wide as rolling hoop that thumps you,
Wide as the wheel a gymnast jumps through,
As gaping as a rotten shoe,
Or thrown net that the light shines through,
As wambly as an unfurled awning,
Or bracelet from a thin arm yawning,
As floppy as an emptied pillow,
Or lax as hobo pants that billow,
As gulping as a pelican
That fish into its pouch does cram.
They claim I fucked her in a pond?
Not so, since her cunt *is* the pond!

## 11.22

You kiss the boys' smooth faces, it is clear,
And their fresh bodies nude you grapple near.
But do not use your hand to work their dick–
That hand is worse for them than is your prick.
To make them play too soon the part of man
Will give them aspirations other than
Are proper to a boy who purely seeks
A sexy coupling proper to smooth cheeks.
For Nature gives us two paths to a boy:
Keep yours, and don't the woman's part annoy.

11.23

She wants to marry me, with some petitions.
But I insist on different conditions:
"You'll get me if you bring me all your fortune,
And if you never sex with me importune.
No bedding we'll have on the wedding night,
And to my mistress I'll retain a right.
Your maid you will concede to my desire,
And watch me with my little boy on fire.
At dinner you may not sit close to me,
Or brush your gown across my sleeve or knee.
You'll kiss me not except upon request,
And then kiss like a grandmother or guest.
If you can meet all these demands, then see
What husband you acquire—it won't be me."

11.24

You are my patron—you demand
That I be always near at hand.
I trot behind you through the town,
Which drives my time for poems down.
Why do I swell (a bit) your train
And see my work go down the drain?
You know my work is often cited.
Important men want me to write it.
The critics praise it, readers laugh,
Yet you cut down my rate by half.
A month goes by, I write no line.
And if you frown, alone I dine.

## 11.25

His cock, so long in service, is not young.
It's time, alas, to mobilize his tongue.

## 11.26

My pretty cupbearer, my tease,
Touch your lips to the wineglass, please.
And if you make my own lips wetter,
Jove's Ganymede was never better.

## 11.28

The doctor's mental patient fucked a lad.
What in that action makes you think him mad?

## 11.29

Your aged claw digs furrows in my dick,
Converts it to a scarred and sorry stick.
If you would warm and moisten me with art,
Give me, of all your holdings, just one part.
Forget your fingers' impotent attack,
For wealth's your only aphrodisiac.

11.35

You dine with hundreds—none I know.
So I come to your table slow.
Why go to eat away from home—
To be, in all that crowd, alone?

11.37

You give yourself such ostentatious gifts—
A ring your finger, struggling, barely lifts.
You do, for ring-size, not a thing by halves;
It would have fit, in your slave days, your calves.

11.38

Say who for such a slave this high price pays?
A deaf man hears not what his master says.

## 11.39

### THE OLD NURSE

You tended me in childhood, I agree,
Made sure of all things that were good for me.
But now my whiskers fall into the basin
And girls say my new whiskers their cheeks chasten.
Yet you keep my expenses in your hand,
And terrify the friends within my band.
You watch me, catch me, scold me all the time
As if there were no minute that is mine.
Should I dress up, or wear a fancy suit,
You reprimand, "Your father would not do't."
You monitor my drinks, down to the least.
I cannot keep a slave who is my priest.
How dare you stand by me with brows that pucker?
Don't you see here my mistress, how I fuck her?

## 11.40

He treasures her, the source of his delight,
But cannot fuck her now, by day or night.
He tells a friend the malady that vexes:
A fever sore his kind of "fucking" hexes.

11.43

You caught me, wife, red-peckered in a boy,
And tell me you've an ass I can enjoy.
But this is what made hapless Juno wonder
Why Jove, instead, rammed Ganymede in thunder.
Great Hercules bent boys instead of bows,
Though his wife had an ass, the whole world knows.
Apollo turned from Daphne to a boy.
Achilles his Patroclus would enjoy,
Though fair Briseis offered him her back.
So, wife of mine, you ask me what you lack?
To your own back you wish me to be shunt?
Yours is no real ass, but a doubled cunt.


11.44

You're old and sick, and no child is your heir.
You ask why everybody seems to care?
When poor you had real friends and had your health.
Now what your clients love is just your wealth.


11.45

When you would in a brothel tarry,
You are of all the peepholes wary.
You do not hide your having girls
Or rosy little boys with curls.
You don't deny an honest fuck.
You hide the kinky ways you suck.

### 11.46

Your dick comes only half-alive in dream
To spit a ludicrous and little stream.
It cannot, waking, find the mark it wants,
But only dribbles feebly down your pants.
Why feebly poke at cunt-hole or at ass,
As if for able man you still could pass?
Your error is in aiming too far south,
The place that you must rise to is the mouth.

### 11.47

Why does he shun bathhouses? Lest he fuck.
Why swim in lonely puddles? Lest he fuck.
Why keep from normal women? Lest he fuck.
Why suck at cunts in secret? Lest he fuck.

### 11.50

The tomb of Virgil was left desolate,
  Not one to honor it came weeping.
But Silius has made it consecrate,
  A poet in a poet's keeping.

### 11.54

You rob a corpse where it is laid,
The incense for the funeral paid.
Feet taught your hands to scoop up pelf—
With your slave feet, you stole yourself.

## 11.55

He says he hopes you'll sire an heir?
You think he really has a care?
Tell him your wife will soon deliver,
He'll have more pangs than birth could give her.
Give him one last and fatal bother–
Tell him, while dying, you're a father.

## 11.58

Just now I have a hard-on for you,
You say intercourse would bore you.
But you, my boy, have lots to buy,
And say the purchaser am I.
Until, you add, you've safely got 'em,
You'll take away your rosy bottom.
But when you issue your petition,
I find myself in this condition–
With razor poised, my barber-slave
Tells me he'll kill instead of shave
If I do not his freedom give.
Of course, I say I want to live.
But once I'm shaved, I will make sure
He's beaten more than he'll endure.
I must do such a thing to you.
But I'll wait till our fuck is through.
When my cock's left with nothing in it,
I'll send you packing, in a minute.

## 11.60

Which whore is best? It is a trying puzzle:
Dora's the beauty, Joan is hot to nuzzle.
Yes, Joan is such a nymphomaniac
That ancient Nestor would not with her lack,
And Pelias would find again his prick,
Which was in dust of ages buried thick.
When Joan has pangs, it is not to deliver—
What doctors hung, not midwives, know to give her.
But Dora is not primed to serve up what you
Desire from women who are not a statue.
All dirty old men would you stun, amaze?
Join Dora's looks with Joan's sex-hungry craze.

## 11.61

His wife gets nothing but his tongue.
He sucks at any girl's front bung.
The madam closes down her door
Before he sips at every whore,
And she will not admit disgrace
Of letting him once kiss her face.
He tells each pregnant woman soon
What babe his tongue finds in her womb.
Vile illness he at last contracts,
Too foul to let him do foul acts.

11.62

Sylvia never gives free lays.
It's never free–because she pays.


11.66

How can the slippery son of a bitch,
With all his vices, not be rich?


11.87

When rich you paid for rosy boys, to pluck 'em.
Now women pay poor you, if you'll just fuck 'em.


11.89

Fresh roses send me not, I like the best
A dead rose, if it died upon your breast.


11.92

To call you bad's not bad enough–
Your labeling must be more tough.
It understates your infamy:
No villain, you–but villainy.


11.93

The poet's house burnt, but not the man.
  Did lazy muses care or know it?
They lost art's opportunity and plan.
  They could have rid us of the poet.

### 11.97

Four times a night I'm good for, but with you
I could not even once in four years screw.

### 11.99

When you rise from a chair, it comes to pass,
That half your skirt is bunched up in your ass.
You pick with this hand, delicate, in vain,
The other hand no more you can restrain.
But still your skirt's imprisoned in the stocks,
Or caught within the epic Clashing Rocks.
To keep from this embarrassment, why then
Just never sit, or never rise again.

### 11.102

They told me you are beautiful. It's true.
So charming if men only look at you.
But what if they could hear you? You'd undo
Whatever else they had believed of you.
Your speech can crumble all your looks away
And make men with you never want to stay.
The only feature that might catch attention
Is what makes people talking statues mention.

### 11.103

So chaste, we can't imagine, even faintly,
How children were begot of one so saintly.

# BOOK TWELVE

### 12.12

You, generous at night when drinking,
Renege by day with clearer thinking.
To make your word worth counting on,
Start drinking at the break of dawn.

### 12.13

Call enmity a fiscal measure–
You'll give away none of your treasure.

### 12.20

Of course we know he'll never wed.
What? Put his sister out of bed?

### 12.23

Your teeth and hair you plainly buy.
Too bad you cannot buy an eye.

12.31

My fields' and fountains' languorous design,
The softly tangled shadows of the vine,
My flame-red roses, to no flower second,
My crops and gardens in all seasons fecund,
The cooling basins where my fishes swim,
The murmuring dovecotes kept in quiet trim—
All these Marcella gave me for a home
To sweeten life when I was gone from Rome.
Should King Alcinous make me his heir,
I'd say I am already free of care.

12.46

You are a pest and sweetheart, hot and cold—
I cannot bear to praise you, or to scold.

12.47

They sell their poems, whether good or not—
Why say that poets are a crazy lot?

12.48

You serve me all expensive foods.
    Am I supposed to pay you back?
It will not work. Exotic goods
    Give me a gout attack.
The dainty oysters soon will be
    The stuff that rags and dogs mop up,
Or left where people stop to pee.
    Why should I then on rare stuffs sup?
To go to banquets of a formal state,
    Or rites with sacred foods complete.
Is nothing I would highly rate,
    Not if a god gave me to eat.
Much better simple fare with friends,
And there the obligation ends.


12.51

Friend Gullible, so often taken in,
Lacks our familiarity with sin.


12.54

In you there's not a single thing to laud.
To turn out honest were your greatest fraud.


12.56

Your ailments have a certain rhythm–
You find surcease in presents given.
All healing comes from gifts laid by.
This time do *us* a favor. Die.

### 12.60

You lie, and drink, and drivel–yet I fawn.
You keep on droning, yet I never yawn.
Bequests will be my payment by and by?
There's just one way to prove it. Die.

### 12.61

You cower, fearful of my caustic verse.
You claim that you could suffer nothing worse.
But fear not. Huge bulls are a lion's prey,
The butterfly can flutter safe away.
For poets who might care to make you grovel,
Seek out some starving scribbler in a hovel.
Find your excoriator in a bar.
You are not good enough to bear my scar.

### 12.65

I offered richest presents for her hug.
But all she said was: "Bring a jug."

### 12.68

You want a patron, and you pester me–
Exactly what made me the City flee.
You're not at some ambitious lawyer's door.
A poet now retired, I'd rather snore.
If Rome you are inflicting on me here,
Then backward to the real one I must steer.

### 12.69

You think that all your friends are fine–
And that your art is genuine.

### 12.73

I'll be your heir, you've often stated.
I'll trust that when it is probated.

### 12.75

One boy of mine prefers the girls.
    Another says he wants to *be* one.
A third his lovely bottom twirls.
    A fourth has charms, but I can't see one.
They all pour scorn on my advances,
    Yet still I struggle to embrace 'em.
For I am forced to take my chances–
    The richest wife could not replace 'em.

### 12.77

Church services had barely started
When with a thunder-stroke he farted.
Men laughed, but angry gods to spite him
Made sure no hosts would now invite him.
Before church to latrines he passes
To empty forcibly his gases.
But even with a cleaned-out gut,
At church he prays with hugged-in butt.

### 12.80

He flatters every person in the place?
There's no one he'll consider a disgrace.

### 12.81

While poor, he pledged me all devotion.
Now rich, of me he has no notion.

### 12.86

What good's a harem of sweet boys,
   And girls all fucking-ready.
If, when you dally with your toys,
   Your prick will not stand steady?

### 12.92

If I were what I am not, rich,
   Would I become a king?
If you were what you are not, brave,
   Would you be anything?

12.97

You have a wife beyond compare–
Rich, loving, learned, fair.
Yet you fuck anywhere but home,
With boys that on the streets do roam.
You buy them with funds from her dowry
And never show her that you're sorry.
When you bring home your labored dick,
She finds it lifeless as a stick.
You have not guarded what you ought.
Has she no right to what she bought?

# BOOK THIRTEEN

## Party Favors (*Xenia*)

Martial gave his first twelve books numbers. The early ones that editors call for convenience Books Thirteen and Fourteen Martial set aside with titles, and he gave a heading (*lemma*) to each of the couplets in the books. The party favors (*xenia*) of Book Thirteen describe the foods the guests were invited to take home after the celebration of the Saturnalian feasts.

## 13.66
**DOVE**

The roasted dove I shall not bite,
Lest Venus of the Doves should smite.

## 13.76
**PEACOCK**

How on meat of peacocks dine,
Whose tails, spread-out, like jewels shine?

## 13.77
**SWAN**

Swan sings its own melodious death
In lingered-out expiring breath.

### 13.81

**TURBOT**

Make you the dish however wide,
The flat-fish flops off every side.

### 13.82

**OYSTERS**

The oyster's had of water quite enough.
Now prime and deck it out with spicier stuff.

### 13.120

**CHEAP WINE**

Better a lesser wine of vintage right
Than famous brands with prices out of sight.

# BOOK FOURTEEN

### Gift Tags (*Apophoréta*)

A s he did for Book Thirteen, Martial gave this book a title, *Gift Tags* (Greek *apophoréta*, literally "carryings off"). He also gave each couplet a heading (*lemma*). The opening verse says that if two lines are too much for anyone to read, just read the heading. These were inscriptions to be written on or by the gifts given during the Saturnalia, some of them to children (who might still have trouble reading). He generally alternates a rich gift with a poor one (like the ivory chest and wooden chest of 14.12 and 14.13).

## 14.2
### THE GIFT TAGS

These lines, read quickly, come in twos—
Read only headings if you choose.

## 14.6
### GIFT NOTEBOOK

This notebook may not cause a celebration,
Till you find here a sexual assignation.

## 14.7
### GIFT NOTEBOOK

This notebook should be taken as a prize,
For love-notes it is just the perfect size.

### 14.9
#### GIFT NOTEBOOK

This notebook may contain your sex accounts,
Or begged sums from your patron, the amounts.

### 14.10
#### GIFT NOTEBOOK

This notebook could have proved the worse
If all preempted by my verse.

### 14.12
#### IVORY CHEST

This ivory box takes only gold,
Put silver in wood boxes old.

### 14.13
#### WOODEN CHEST

This wood box does no treasure hold.
The thing itself?—the whole gift's told.

### 14.14
#### GAME TOKENS

I give you dice, a rich gift maybe—
Depends on what result their play be.

## 14.25
### A COMB

This comb so well articulated
Is useless to the empty-pated.

## 14.26
### WIG

Your wig is made of German hair.
Things foreign are so debonair.

## 14.27
### HAIR DYE

If you would not be white at all,
Why not accept a deep-dyed fall?

## 14.28
### PARASOL

With sun or wind against you sent,
Accept, for very little spent,
A good perambulating tent.

## 14.29
### HAT

At theater this hat's wide brim
Keeps sunshine out and scenery in.

### 14.30
**SPEAR**

To stab a bear or lion grim,
Just keep your arm in aiming trim.

### 14.31
**KNIFE**

Your hunting spear should you throw wide,
Thrust this into the bear, inside.

### 14.34
**SCYTHE**

Our Ruler brings us peace again.
My scythe now harvests wheat, not men.

### 14.36
**BARBER'S TOOLS**

These tools will barb you, clip you, shave–
So all in your emporium save.

### 14.37
**BOOKCASE**

Cram me tight with volumes stout,
I'll keep the worms and cobwebs out.

### 14.39
#### BEDROOM LAMP

No matter how your bedsprings rattle,
I your lamp will never tattle.

### 14.54
#### A RATTLE

For child who is a pesty crier,
This rattle serves as pacifier.

### 14.55
#### A WHIP

This whip will not at all prove able
On horses of an ill-kept stable.

### 14.56
#### TOOTHPASTE

I help along young girls' adventures.
What good can I do old men's dentures?

### 14.57
#### HAIR OIL

This hair oil makes hair stand out tall,
Something no epic lines recall.

## 14.58
### MEDICINE

You lack Greek etymology?
It's time to learn philology.

## 14.59
### PERFUME

Gilead's balm, men's shaving lotion.
Subtler perfume is lady's notion.

## 14.60
### STRETCH MARKS LOTION

This can your belly's wrinkles smooth away
For going to the public baths by day.

## 14.66
### BREAST BAND

Your boobs exceed a hammock's deep confines.
You need a county's spreading boundary lines.

## 14.75
### NIGHTINGALE

Raped Philomela's tuneless tongueless wrong
Is turned to nightingale's eternal song.

### 14.76
**MAGPIE**

I chatter so I cannot be unheard.
Unseen, you would not take me for a bird.

### 14.77
**IVORY CAGE**

A precious bird can here be kept
Like that for which Catullus wept.

### 14.79
**SLAVE WHIPS**

These chastisers are locked away,
But only for the holiday.

### 14.80
**RODS**

Your schoolmaster does this desire,
The wand that held Prometheus' fire.

### 14.81
**POUCH**

This bag would with no Cynic beggar slouch
Or be a poor philosopher's street couch.

## 14.86
**SADDLE**

Saddle your fiery mount with class
Or end up with an aching ass.

## 14.91
**ELEPHANT TUSKS**

To gore a bull these tusks were able,
That now, as legs, uphold a table.

## 14.111
**CRYSTAL**

If, nervous, you fine crystal prize too much,
Your trembling hands may fumble as they touch.

## 14.134
**BRASSIERE**

Sash, tuck her ample bosom in,
That I may stroke her plumped-up skin.

## 14.149
**SCARF**

I care to wrap no giantess's breast.
Let me against a girl's white buds take rest.

## 14.151
### SASH

This sash can circle you if you stay slender.
But if you fatten up—return to sender.

## 14.165
### LYRE

Eurydice with this lyre's song did glow.
But hasty looking doomed her back below.

## 14.166
### LYRE

Played badly, this can get musicians hissed.
In Orpheus' hands, though, beasts and forests list.

## 14.167
### PLECTRUM

Lest lyre string harden your soft thumb,
Take this firm pick and with it thrum.

## 14.174
### HERMAPHRODITE

He entered water one sex, came out two,
His mother and his father blended through.

### 14.194
#### LUCAN

"Your poems are just empty noise"–
    A tale you're always telling.
Then what are all these published "toys"
    The dealer in my books keeps selling?

### 14.197
#### DWARF MULES

Ride these, and safe you will be found,
Secure as you were sitting on the ground.

### 14.203
#### DANCING GIRL

Such sexy dances does she innovate
That purity itself must masturbate.

### 14.205
#### BOY

Give me a boy who needs no shaving
And what's the point of women having?

### 14.206
#### VENUS' GIRDLE

This scarf could beauteous Venus claim,
It will my boy's dear features frame.

# ACKNOWLEDGMENTS

I owe gratitude to my editor, Carolyn Carlson, for support; to my agent, Andrew Wylie, for guidance; to my wife, Natalie, for inspiration; and to the Grand Hotel la Minerve in Rome and the Grand Hotel Continental in Siena, where most of these translations were made.

# PARTIAL INDEX OF SUBJECTS TREATED

## BALDNESS

2.66

6.12

6.57

10.83

12.23

## BANQUETING

| | |
|---|---|
| 3.27 | 9.35 |
| 5.47 | 9.77 |
| 5.50 | 9.89 |
| 6.48 | 12.48 |
| 8.6 | |

## BODY ODOR

2.12

3.55

6.98

## CUNNILINGUS

| | |
|---|---|
| 1.77 | 11.40 |
| 2.84 | 11.45 |
| 3.81 | 11.46 |
| 3.88 | 11.47 |
| 9.67 | 11.61 |

## DEBT DELINQUENCY

## FELLATIO

## LEGACY HUNTING

## MARITAL FIDELITY

## MARITAL INFIDELITY

| | |
|---|---|
| 2.43 | 2.83 |
| 2.56 | 3.26 |
| 2.60 | 6.90 |

## MISOGYNY

| | | |
|---|---|---|
| 1.34 | 4.20 | 7.75 |
| 1.62 | 5.43 | 10.90 |
| 1.64 | 5.45 | 11.21 |
| 2.52 | 6.23 | 11.99 |
| 2.73 | 6.98 | |
| 3.72 | 7.18 | |

## PEDERASTY

| | | |
|---|---|---|
| 1.58 | 8.46 | 11.26 |
| 2.49 | 8.63 | 11.28 |
| 3.65 | 9.21 | 11.43 |
| 4.42 | 9.25 | 11.58 |
| 5.46 | 9.56 | 11.87 |
| 7.59 | 10.42 | 12.75 |
| 7.62 | 11.22 | 12.97 |

## TRIBUTES TO THE DEAD

| PRIVATE FIGURES | PUBLIC FIGURES |
|---|---|
| 5.34 | 1.42 |
| 5.37 | 3.66 |
| 6.52 | 5.71 |
| 9.76 | 5.74 |
| 10.53 | 11.13 |
| 10.63 | 11.50 |

## WINE

| | |
|---|---|
| 1.11 | 3.57 |
| 1.18 | 5.4 |
| 1.28 | 9.98 |
| 1.56 | 10.30 |
| 1.71 | 12.12 |
| 1.87 | |

## THE WRITING PROFESSION